The Chartered Institute of Management Accountants

The Chartered Institute of Management Accountants

CIMA

Publishing

Accounting for Risk in the NHS

Paul Fenn

Stephen Diacon

Ron Hodges

Pamela Watson

University of Nottingham Business School

This publication arises from the research project 'Accounting for Risk in the NHS' which was funded with a research grant from the CIMA Research Foundation. The award of a Research Foundation grant, and the publication of findings in this format, indicates that the recipient has successfully passed two separate peer review processes, which also involved practitioner assessors. The views expressed in this publication are the authors' own, and do not necessarily represent those of CIMA.

Acknowledgements

The authors of this report wish to thank the following persons and organisations for assistance during this project:

- The director of corporate affairs of an NHS trust for general encouragement and for allowing access to trust records and personnel during the first stage of the project.
- The risk manager, claims manager and management accountant of an NHS trust who provided considerable time and assistance during the first stage of the project.
- The directors of finance, management accountants and claims managers of twelve NHS trusts who gave us their time, expertise and views during the interviews in the second stage of the project.
- The managers in various NHS trusts who commented upon an early draft of the questionnaire and/or took time to answer the questions in the final version during the third stage of the project.
- The Research Foundation of the Chartered Institute of Management Accountants for the provision of funding for the project.

First published in 2000 by:
The Chartered Institute of Management Accountants
63 Portland Place
London
W1N 4AB

ISBN 1 85971 349 1

Contents

	Executive Summary	v
	Introduction	1
1	***Background and Literature Review***	3
	1.1 Management of claims in NHS trusts	3
	1.2 Risk allocation and the role of insurance in NHS trusts	5
	1.3 Accounting for claims in NHS trusts	8
2	***Research Method***	13
	2.1 Introduction	13
	2.2 Stage 1: Procedure and documentation review at an NHS hospital	13
	2.3 Stage 2: Interviews with managers	14
	2.4 Stage 3: Questionnaire design, distribution and analysis	16
3	***Research Findings***	19
	3.1 Management and administrative structures	19
	3.2 Estimating the likelihood of liability and quantum	21
	3.3 Determining accounting provisions and contingencies	26
	3.4 Treatment in NHS trusts' budgets	29
	3.5 Allocation in NHS trusts' management accounts	31
	3.6 Recovery of costs in prices	32
	3.7 Insurance arrangements	35
	3.8 Number and value of claims	41
4	***Summary, Conclusions and Recommendations***	45
	Appendices	49
	References	79

Executive Summary

This report describes the findings of a research study into the accounting and financial implications of clinical negligence, employers' liability and public liability claims on hospital trusts. It includes extracts from interviews with finance directors, management accountants and claims managers at twelve NHS trusts together with the results of a questionnaire sent to all hospital trusts in England.

It is apparent that trusts face an increasing financial risk from the cumulative growth in legal liabilities arising from activities since their formation. Once claims are made, there remains a significant degree of uncertainty over whether and when a claim will settle, and at what cost to the trust.

The extent to which trusts transfer the claims management and claims financing roles to insurers or the NHSLA is partly a matter of managerial discretion, and partly a matter of the conditions imposed by the insurers. There are adverse incentives present due to the lack of true experience rating for CNST cover.

There are considerable variations in accounting practice for those liabilities that are retained rather than transferred to insurers:

- The description of likelihood of liability used by trusts varied and was most commonly influenced by descriptions provided by trust solicitors. Many claims are assessed at '50 per cent' or 'medium' likelihood of liability. Practice varies as to whether any claim which is assigned such a probability should be provided in full, or partially or not at all.
- Most trusts determine the aggregate of their accounting provision as the sum of provisions on individual claims while a minority adjust the aggregate of provisions, making reference to 'prudence' and 'realism' as a justification for doing so. Some trusts were prepared to omit liabilities from the provision on the grounds that the quantum could not be assessed with reasonable accuracy.
- No trust in our sample made provision for incurred but not reported (IBNR) claims.
- Some claims are assigned a probability of 0 per cent by trusts, implying that the claim would not be paid under any circumstances. Nevertheless, almost 40 per cent of trusts reported that they would still disclose some or all of these amounts as contingent liabilities.
- The costs of insurance premiums and uninsured losses relating to claims are, almost invariably, treated as central overheads within a trust rather than being assigned to particular clinical activities.

The lack of consistency in measuring these liabilities may hinder performance comparisons between trusts and creates uncertainty in the interpretation of the consolidated accounts of the NHS. A closer liaison between trust solicitors, claims managers and accountants is needed to ensure the claims are considered on a case by case basis and that liability and quantum estimates are updated regularly. In the longer term, as their claims experience builds, trusts should work towards the creation of a claims database held locally and also pooled nationally through the NHSLA.

Introduction

In common with all organisations, the National Health Service (NHS) is subject to uncertainty in the outcomes of its activities. The existence of uncertainties in predicting the outcome of events is commonly referred to as 'risk'. Baldwin (1997, p.2) defines risk as 'the probability that a particular adverse event will occur during a stated period of time', making clear that risk involves an assessment of the likelihood of occurrence of a particular event. In an accounting context, the Accounting Standards Board (ASB, 1994, para. 5) defines risk as 'Uncertainty as to the amount of benefits. The term includes both potential for gain and exposure to loss,' suggesting that measurement of risk results in the recognition of gains or losses from changes of quantum used in accounting reports.

This report summarises the findings of a research project that examines accounting issues arising from claims made on NHS hospital trusts (trusts) by patients, staff and members of the public. Such claims may result in trusts making payments for clinical negligence, employer liability or public liability.

At the individual trust level, the allegations surrounding a claim may not be well founded and uncertainty exists as to whether a payment will be made or should be anticipated. If it is expected that a claim will result in a compensation payment there is uncertainty of the quantum to provide in accounting reports. If a compensation payment is not expected it is still necessary to consider whether a claim should be included within accounting reports as a contingent liability and, if so, at what quantum. Accounting for these claims in a consistent manner will provide information to assist the claims management process and provide a basis for measuring the likely and potential financial impact on trusts. Trust accounting data is also important in the negotiation of pricing and funding arrangements with commissioners.

Nationally, the consolidation of trust financial statements into the NHS accounts should provide information to assist policy development and implementation. However, the determination of these costs appears to have been complicated by the formation of separate accounting entities in the NHS adopting different accounting policies. For example, the Comptroller and Auditor General reported a variety of practices of accounting for clinical negligence in the NHS (England) accounts for 1995/96 (NAO, 1997). Provisions of trusts were shown net of anticipated assistance from the NHS Litigation Authority (NHSLA) (para. 61) while the NHSLA accounts contained no provisions because 'no liabilities had been passed from the trusts to the Authority' (para. 91). Only 41 of 105 health authorities had made a realistic provision (para. 77), and £84.5 million of provisions had been excluded from the summarised accounts to 'enable them to be prepared on a consistent basis' (para. 78).

There has been a series of increasingly vague and imprecise estimates of the overall cost of these claims to the NHS (see Towse and Danzon, 1999). For example, the recent headline figure of £2.8 billion in respect of clinical negligence

(*Independent,* 10 May 1999) is based upon estimates of the potential liability, including those from incidents not yet reported, given by the Comptroller and Auditor General (NAO, 1999).

The research for this report was conducted by members of the University of Nottingham Business School (UNBS) and sponsored by the Research Foundation of the Chartered Institute of Management Accountants (CIMA). The key research objectives were as follows:

- to determine the role of accounting and finance personnel in assessing and quantifying the risks relating to clinical negligence, and employers' and public liability claims;
- to identify the extent to which the management and reporting of these risks is transferred through insurance contracts and pooling of risk arrangements;
- to identify how the cost of risk retained by trusts is represented in their internal and external accounting reports and the processes followed to estimate these costs;
- to identify how trusts go about funding the impact of these costs.

The research was carried out in three stages.

Stage 1: a detailed review of procedures and documentation within a large NHS general hospital. The primary purpose of this stage was to provide the research team with an understanding of the processes involved in the reporting and recording of claims to inform later stages of the project.

Stage 2: a series of interviews with finance directors, accountants and claims managers in twelve hospital trusts throughout England. The objective was to obtain qualitative evidence of the procedures adopted by trusts in identifying and quantifying their liabilities. It also provided examples of differences in accounting practices that informed the design of the questionnaire used in the third stage of the project.

Stage 3: the distribution of a questionnaire sent to the director of finance of 221 trusts in England to obtain an understanding of the methods of accounting for these liabilities over a wider selection of hospital trusts in order to provide a basis for quantitative analysis and to complement the earlier work.

The second section of this report provides a background to the management of clinical negligence, employers' and public liability claims in trusts, the role of insurance in the allocation of risk from these claims, and the related accounting issues. The third section describes the methods adopted by the research team in each of the three phases of the project. The fourth section presents the detailed findings from the project. Conclusions and recommendations are presented in the final section.

1

Background and Literature Review

1.1 Management of claims in NHS trusts

A typical trust is subject to a number of claims by patients, employees and the public over alleged negligence leading to personal injury. A claim is initiated when a letter is received from the claimant or the claimant's solicitor mentioning the possibility of legal action and a demand for compensation.[1] The allegations may not be well founded, and the size of any award of compensation may be difficult to predict. A number of issues complicate the management of, and accounting for, such claims. There may be a considerable delay between the timing of the event that gives rise to the claim (medical treatment or an accident) and the claim being made by the claimant or his or her representative. There may then be a further delay between notification of the claim and its eventual settlement or abandonment. Information is exchanged during this period including, if relevant, the claimant's medical records, expert reports, and witness statements. Some claims will be abandoned, while others will continue to formal legal proceedings following the issue of a writ. Offers of settlement may be made at any stage of this process.

The likelihood at any given time that the claim is dropped, settled out of court or tried is, to some extent, in the hands of the trust itself. The term 'claims management' may be used to capture the means by which this process is handled by trusts.[2] Most hospital trusts now employ at least one individual with a claims management role. These managers are often to be found within a legal services or litigation department. The solicitors of a trust are usually given the task of representing it in any legal proceedings, and they also play a significant role in the handling of each claim. However, the extent to which trusts defer to their solicitors on matters of valuation and strategy, rather than rely on in-house claims managers' expertise, varies considerably from one trust to another (Dowding, 1996). As the claims management role has become more complex, the need for adequate training is being addressed, and there is now an association dedicated to improving the skills and training of NHS claims handlers: the Asso-

1 Trusts typically adopt separate procedures for complaints.

2 This is distinct from, or perhaps a subcategory of, the risk management function within trusts, which would have as one of its objectives the reduction of the number of both clinical and non-clinical adverse events which lead to legal claims being initiated. This wider function is outside the scope of this project, which is concerned with the means adopted to manage the risks associated with claims once they have arisen. However, the information generated by claims managers would be expected to feed back into the wider risk management process.

ciation of Litigation and Risk Managers (ALARM). Moreover, claims management experience has gradually been introduced to the NHS from the commercial insurance industry, with the result that the issue of litigation risk has been extended beyond the narrow confines of clinical negligence alone (Walshe and Dineen, 1998).

There is a growing body of literature that has explored empirically the disposition of medical negligence claims brought against hospitals; much of this literature is American (Hughes and Savoca, 1997; Sloan and Hoerger, 1991; Farber and White, 1991, 1994). Some research on English data has recently been forthcoming (Fenn and Rickman, 1999). A recent research report to the Lord Chancellor's Department drawing on the same data showed that, of 3,749 cases in a database drawn from several trusts, 2,850 had been closed, settled and/or archived by January 1999 (LCD, 1999). Damages had been paid in only 672 (24 per cent) of these cases. The mean time from the incident to a claim beginning was 1,066 days, and the mean time from a claim beginning to the closure of the case was 1,004 days. These figures, taken together, illustrate both the 'long tail' nature of litigation against trusts and the uncertainty over whether or not a claim will ultimately result in financial liability. For these reasons, claims managers typically attempted to make an estimate of each claim's value, taking into account information provided to them by the claimant. These estimates were then revised over time as more information became available. On average, these claims had an initial expected value of £40,783 rising to £48,854 at the final revision. At the same time, claims managers also made a judgement in relation to the likelihood that the plaintiff would win in court. Again, this judgement may be revised as more evidence becomes available through expert reports and witness statements. Table 1.1 gives the breakdown of these estimates.

Table 1.1 Estimates of liability by NHS claims managers (LCD, 1999)

	First estimate		*Last estimate*	
	Frequency	*%*	*Frequency*	*%*
Liable	217	9.3	391	17.2
Probably liable	32	1.4	21	0.9
Poorly defensible	233	10.0	229	10.1
Probably defensible	305	13.1	371	16.3
Defensible	193	8.3	177	7.8
Not liable	253	10.8	521	22.9
Probably not liable	35	1.5	27	1.2
Unclear	926	39.6	397	17.5
Case closed	66	2.8	140	6.2
Missing	77	3.3	0	0.0
Total	2337	100.0	2274	100.0

The most striking feature of this table is the way in which estimates of liability change over the course of the claim, such that, of 40 per cent of cases that begin with an assessment of 'unclear' liability, most evolve to an estimate that the trust is 'liable' or 'not liable'.[3] It is this process by which claims managers make estimates of the likelihood that a claim will be paid, and the cost to the trust if it is paid, which is the focus of this project. In particular, we were interested to explore the interrelationship between claims managers' estimates, and the use made of these estimates in the financial and management accounting procedures.

1.2 Risk allocation and the role of insurance in NHS trusts

In investigating the impact on trusts of possible claims for personal injury arising from clinical negligence, employers' liability and public liability, the various methods of transferring and financing such liabilities need to be taken into account. This is because the decision to transfer these liabilities to a third party naturally impacts on income and expenditure accounts (I&E) and balance sheets, on cash control, and therefore on the achievement of financial targets. It can also influence prices charged to providers. In general, potential liability can be retained (in whole or in part) by trusts, may be transferred to external commercial insurers, or may be pooled among various trusts.

Trusts typically handle their liabilities in different ways. By far the majority of trusts now part-finance their clinical negligence liabilities via membership of the Clinical Negligence Scheme for Trusts (CNST). The CNST operates as a pay-as-you-go risk pool, where the annual contributions are set at the level required to meet the outflow – in terms of claims paid plus expenses – in each year. In contrast to commercial insurance, the CNST does not fund current contributions in a loss reserve in order to meet liabilities which have been incurred in the current accounting period but have not yet been paid.

On the other hand, the financing of employers' liability and public liability claims is currently dealt with via the purchase of commercial insurance contracts. However, in October 1998 it was announced that trusts should no longer insure these non-clinical risks commercially (NHSE, 1998c), and from 1 April 1999 these were to be placed with a risk pool operated by the NHSLA (NHSE, 1999d).

In the financial years 1991/92 to 1994/95, trusts were liable in full for the costs of claims relating to medical treatment from the year when the trust was formed. However, the CNST was created in April 1995 as a mutual risk pool, which received contributions from member trusts to finance clinical negligence costs. Currently, more than 95 per cent of trusts are CNST members (NHSE, 1998d). The liability risk

---

3 It should be noted that this classification of liability estimates is specific to the trusts concerned. Other classifications, such as those based on percentage estimates, are commonly adopted elsewhere.

from claims relating to medical treatment prior to April 1995 initially remained with individual trusts, but from April 1996 these risks have been covered through the NHSLA under what became known as the Existing Liability Scheme (ELS).

Contributions to the CNST depend on four main criteria:

- which of four categories of services a trust provides;
- trust turnover;
- the choice of excess level; and
- trust ability to meet certain risk management standards.

Both the CNST and the ELS require trusts to accept an excess for smaller claims and to share risks up to an ultimate threshold. The excess levels and ultimate thresholds are shown in Table 1.2. However, discussions with trusts indicate that there has been some relaxation of the excess levels for the CNST, and several trusts have opted recently to reduce them.

It is worth noting that the long tail of clinical negligence liabilities means that the CNST will have to increase its claims outlay (and hence its annual premium contribution rate) for several years before reaching a 'steady state'. However, membership of the CNST is voluntary, and trusts may have some discretion over their participation via their choice of excess. There is therefore the very real possibility that trusts which see themselves as low risk may wish to pull back their involvement with the CNST in future in order to avoid having to pay for the claims of those with poor claims and risk management.

Table 1.2 Allocation of financial risk for clinical negligence claims

Scheme	*Excess*	*Ultimate threshold*
ELS	£10,000	£500,000
CNST	Between £10,000 and £500,000	Between £100,000 and £1,000,000
Allocation of risk	*NHS trust*	*ELS or CNST*
Up to the excess level	100%	0%
From excess level to ultimate threshold	20%	80%
Above the ultimate threshold	0%	100%

The purchase of commercial insurance and/or participation in mutual risk pools such as the CNST provides trusts with a package of interrelated services:

- ***Risk transfer***. For the payment of a suitable contribution or premium, part of the liability can be transferred from the trust's balance sheet to that of the insurer (although trusts are required to report provisions and contingencies both gross and net of insurance recoveries). Of course, the trust balance sheet will still need to reflect the uninsured part of these liabilities – depending on the size and frequency of losses and on the nature of the partial insurance arrangements. In the case of clinical negligence, although the liability on the trust balance sheet is reduced to the extent that it can recover from the NHSLA, there is no corresponding transfer to the NHSLA balance sheet.

In general, the ability to transfer liabilities to the balance sheet of an external insurer has public policy benefits because it provides an assurance to injured third parties that the monies will be available to make compensation payments. This is because the liabilities of insurance companies are not just accounting entries but have to be funded and backed by real and financial assets. Furthermore, insurance companies are required to maintain an excess of assets over liabilities (the minimum 'solvency margin') which is monitored by government. In the case of medical negligence, liabilities to injured patients do not appear in the balance sheet of the NHSLA, but are ultimately underwritten by the taxpayer.

Similarly, risk transfer allows a trust to reduce fluctuations in its I&E by replacing the random impact of claims paid with a (hopefully) more stable premium contribution.

- ***Risk distribution.*** The fundamental principle of insurance and risk pooling is that the losses of the few should be paid by the many so that claims payments are met from the accumulated contributions of all the customers/members. If total payments exceed accumulated contributions then the excess must either be met from free reserves, in the case of an insurance company, or by raising additional contributions in the case of a pay-as-you-go risk pool.
- ***Risk financing.*** Membership of a risk pool or the purchase of insurance guarantees access to finance which can partly or wholly offset the cash outlay involved in a claims payment. Since a trust is cash limited, and cannot carry cash reserves, the provision of a financing arrangement enables it to avoid having either to divert cash from other sources, such as maintenance or patient care, or to increase its borrowing.
- ***Cost-effective administrative and advisory services.*** Commercial insurers and risk pools will generally provide their customers with technical, actuarial and specialist legal services. A key feature of liability insurance is that, once a claim has been notified, the insurer will usually take over the negotiations with injured third parties. In theory, a trust has the option to hire its own claims management and legal services instead of relying on those provided by insurers. However, it may be advantageous to utilise the services of external insurers if they can obtain economies of scale and specialisation. Furthermore, external insurers have a strong incentive to offer quality advice and legal services because these will also serve to reduce their own claims payments.[4]
- ***Incentives to manage risk.*** In general, insurance or pooling can dilute the incentive to manage risk as the costs of risk management have to be paid by the trust, while the benefits accrue to the insurer/pool. The situation can be

4 It is unclear whether the same incentive applies to pay-as-you-go risk pools, since higher than expected claims outlays are financed via increased contributions from all pool members.

improved if the premium contributions are related to the risk (although this is diluted if premium reductions are deferred) and if the insurance only provides partial cover. The same problem can emerge at a sub-unit level if clinical directorates have to meet their risk management costs while the benefits (in the form of lower liability payments or premium contributions) accrue to the trust and are not allocated down to directorates.

- ***Investment income.*** In competitive insurance markets, premiums will be discounted in order to allow for any investment income earned on the insurer's technical reserves.[5] This enables trusts to benefit from the expertise of the insurer's investment department. On the other hand, few such benefits arise from pay-as-you-go risk pools such as the CNST because there are no technical reserves to invest.

1.3 Accounting for claims in NHS trusts

This section of the report reviews the policies and results of accounting for claims by trusts from 1991 to 1998. It concentrates on claims against trusts in respect of clinical negligence since such claims tend to be more costly, in aggregate, than public or employers' liability claims. The costs of clinical negligence are required to be disclosed in the full accounts of each trust to comply with the *NHS Trust Manual of Accounts,* and this enables the costs to be tracked over this period. However, the principles of accounting for provisions and contingencies also apply to employers' and public liability claims.

Trusts are required to adopt an accruals-based system for financial reporting. Financial targets of trusts, over this period, included making a return before interest charges of 6 per cent of average net assets, breaking even after interest and public dividend payments and maintaining borrowings within an external funding limit (EFL). Costs reported in the income and expenditure account (I&E) will reduce the net income of the trust and its net assets in the balance sheet, while payments will contribute towards the closing EFL position. The accounting treatment of claims can therefore have a direct impact upon the ability of a trust to meet its financial targets.

Three issues arise when reporting the cost of claims in trust accounts:

- Amounts paid in a financial year for claims will be treated as costs in the I&E, unless these costs have been provided for in an earlier year.
- At the end of each financial year it is necessary for trusts to estimate the cost of those claims for which no payment has yet been made but for which it is thought probable that payments will be made in the future. This adds to the costs reported in the I&E and is treated as a provision for future liabilities in the trust balance sheet.
- At the end of each financial year it is necessary for trusts to estimate the cost of those claims for which it is thought probable that no payment will be made in

5 So long as the rate of return on invested funds exceeds the inflation rate of liability awards.

the future. Although not recognised in the I&E or the balance sheet, this quantum is required to be disclosed in a note as a contingent liability.

For the purposes of external financial reporting, the financial results of trusts are determined broadly on equivalent commercial accounting practice (see, for example, NHSE 1997, Ch. 8). In the context of claims, trusts were expected to comply with the requirements of SSAP 18, *Accounting for Contingencies* (ASC, 1980) during the period covered by our analysis. SSAP 18 was withdrawn in 1998 and replaced by FRS 12, *Provisions and Contingencies* (ASB, 1998). Implementation of FRS 12 in trust accounts has been deferred until 1999/2000 (NHSE, 1999c).

Table 1.3 illustrates the trend of clinical negligence I&E charges, provisions and contingent liabilities from April 1991 to March 1998. Over this period, the financial responsibility for claims was transferred from health authorities to an increasing number of trusts. Interpretation of the trend is also complicated by the formation of the CNST in 1995 and the changing accounting regulations imposed on trusts throughout this period.

Table 1.3 Clinical negligence charges and liabilities of NHS trusts in England (£m)

Year ended 31 March	*I&E charges*	*Balance sheet net provisions*	*Net contingent liabilities*	*Gross contingent liabilities*
1992	1.2	1.0	2.4	2.4
1993	2.2	2.3	24.9	24.9
1994	7.0	7.3	91.0	91.0
1995	26.3	30.4	228.1	228.1
1996	43.9	87.4	192.5	326.6
1997	72.7	135.6	191.2	609.3
1998	84.9	173.1	237.0	799.3

Sources: Individual accounts of trusts and *Fitzhugh Directories* (HCIS 1995–9).

Several factors contribute to the relatively low level of I&E costs from 1991/92 to 1994/95. First, it took a number of years for provider units throughout England to gain trust status, the total increasing from 57 to 419 over this period. Second, the reluctance to accrue for future claims reflects the long tail nature of these liabilities and the many uncertainties that lie between receipt and closure of the claim. The absence of reliable claims data on which to base estimates of the likelihood of settlement amounts at this early stage of the claims management process discouraged trusts from making early, and possibly excessive, provision. Third, a trust was allowed to limit its provision to 0.5 per cent of turnover on the grounds that it could finance large clinical negligence claims through a loan scheme and treat the payment as deferred expenditure. This accounting treatment contravened SSAP 18, which required that losses should be accrued 'where it is probable that a future event will confirm a loss which can be estimated with reasonable accuracy' (para. 15).

The NHS Executive provided little guidance to encourage a consistent approach to reporting these provisions during this period. For example, the 1994 edition of the

NHS Trust Manual of Accounts (NHSE, 1994, p.39.4) did not include advice on how a trust might determine its provision for clinical negligence costs. The illustrative trust balance sheet (Appendix A1.5) included no heading for provisions. The statement of accounting policies for clinical negligence costs (Appendix A1.10) described the 0.5 per cent limit, deferred expenditure within debtors, the amortisation of loans, and interest, but made no mention of provisions or accruals for unpaid costs. In contrast, the *Manual* provided a detailed example of how to account for loan finance obtained to cover clinical negligence costs, although no trusts had such loans. The impression given is that the NHS Executive had little concern over the application of accruals accounting at this time: instead, there was a fixation on the cash funding of clinical negligence costs. Important as this is, it ignores the impact that unpaid costs may have on a trust's reported earnings and financial position.

The 1996 version of the *NHS Trusts Manual of Accounts* issued under FDL(96)07 (NHSE, 1996a) included amended rules on accounting for clinical negligence claims. Provisions could no longer be limited to 0.5 per cent of turnover, as all liabilities that were expected to be paid and that could be estimated with reasonable certainty had to be fully provided. These changes separated the cash-flow effect from the charging of these costs against revenue. Under these amended accounting rules, trusts were instructed that the cost of claims relating to incidents prior to 1 April 1995 and not previously provided, were to be recognised as an adjustment to the opening provision rather than as an I&E cost of 1995/96. In contrast, previously accrued liabilities that were now covered by the CNST and ELS schemes were to be credited to the I&E in 1996. A total of £21.7 million was added to clinical negligence provisions at the start of 1995/96 under these arrangements (Hodges, 1999).

A strict interpretation of FDL(96)07 implied that even a claim for which the risk of payment was thought to be remote would need to be assessed and included in contingent liabilities. The requirement to disclose a value for all claims, however spurious, could result in a misleadingly high indicator of the risk exposure of trusts. A large majority of negligence claims received by the NHS do not lead to a payment to the claimant (Fenn and Dingwall, 1991), but trusts could only avoid this accounting disclosure on the grounds that including these contingencies would make the accounts misleading.

The NHS Executive attempted, once again, to clarify the treatment of clinical negligence costs in 1997 under FDL(97)13 (NHSE, 1997). Provisions were required to be calculated on a case-by-case basis, and an offset (under the CNST or ELS rules) could be shown if the NHSLA did not dispute its liability (para. 17.15.4). For the first time the *Manual* stated explicitly that material contingent liabilities should only be disclosed where they are *not* accrued or provided for in the accounts (para. 17.20.1), although a potential liability might be split into two parts with one part accrued or provided for and the second part disclosed. The accounting treatment specified depended upon the estimated likelihood of outcome as specified in Table 1.4.

Table 1.4 Accounting treatment of clinical negligence liabilities, 1996/97

Likelihood of outcome	*Probability*	*Accounting treatment*
Reasonably certain	Over 95%	Accrue: do not disclose in the note of contingent liabilities.
Probable	95% to 50%	Where the amount can be estimated with reasonable accuracy: provide and do not disclose in the note of contingent liabilities. Where the amount cannot be estimated with reasonable accuracy: do not provide; disclose in the note of contingent liabilities.
Possible but not probable and remote	50% to 0%	Disclose in the note of contingent liabilities: do not provide or accrue.

Source: NHS Trust Manual of Accounts (March 1997), n. 17.20.3.

Additional guidance required the accounting costs for clinical negligence to reflect the amounts stated in schedules issued by the NHSLA unless a trust could justify otherwise to its auditors. There still remained a potential conflict that a probability of close to 0 per cent in the table would seem to be equivalent to a remote likelihood, and therefore did not require disclosure as a contingency. It is also apparent from Table 1.4 that the assignment of a probability of future payment to each claim becomes a critical part of the application of these accounting rules. An assigned probability of more than 50 per cent requires the cost to be accrued, whereas an assignment of less than 50 per cent does not. The treatment of a claim that is assigned a probability of exactly 50 per cent is unclear, as it appears possible to place it into either category or, perhaps, to split the claim to fall equally into both.

The fieldwork for this research report was completed before the publication of trust accounts for 1998/99, and prior to the issue of recent NHSE guidance on accounting for claims in the 1999/2000 financial statements of trust and health authorities. Accounting for clinical negligence liabilities in 1998/99 continues to be based upon SSAP 18 (NHSE, 1998b, para. 16.279), and the application of FRS 12 by trusts has been deferred until 1999/2000. However, trusts are required to report what their provisions and contingencies *would have been* had FRS 12 applied to 1998/99 accounts (NHSE, 1999a). The calculation is made in the following manner:

(a) Taking 75 per cent of those claims (with a probability of payment between 50 per cent and 100 per cent) which are presently provided in full;

(b) Add 25 per cent of those claims (with a probability of payment between 0 per cent and 50 per cent) which are presently not provided for at all;

(c) Deduct 25 per cent of the net opening provision to bring it down from 100 per cent to 75 per cent provision.

This calculation is based upon the use of an expected-value concept. It assumes that there is a 75 per cent mean of the probability distribution of claims in category *(a)* and *(c)*, and a 25 per cent mean for category *(b)*. The guidance fails to clarify what should happen to claims with a 50 per cent probability of payment, which could still be placed into either category *(a)* or *(b)*. It is also apparent that the calculation represents a simplification of the true probability distributions; for example, the provision will be overstated if remote contingent liabilities are included in category *(c)* and which cause 25 per cent of such remote contingencies to be included in the provision!

HSC 1999/146 (NHSE, 1999b) provides that costs which are 'non-cash-impacting' (para. 13) will not be taken into account when determining if a trust has met its break-even obligation, but also states (para. 14) that there should be no such distortions because of the strict enforcement of 'back-to-back' provisions required under HSC 1998/105 (NHSE, 1998a).

HSC 1999/174 (NHSE, 1999c) requires the accounts of trusts and health authorities for the financial year 1999/2000 to comply fully with FRS 12. All clinical negligence claims should be provided for, calculated using an expected-value concept and discounted to present value if its effect is material (para. 14). A further extension of the provisioning process is the requirement that a provision should be made where a reliable estimate can be made of the total value of 'IBNR cases' (Annex C, para. 4). These represent liabilities that have been incurred as a result of the occurrence of clinical incidents, but where claims have yet to be reported. Provisions for claims are required to be disclosed as gross liabilities, with any expected recoveries from the NHSLA being disclosed as assets in trust balance sheets, while the net cost is disclosed as expenditure in the income and expenditure account.

It can be seen that numerous changes to the accounting regulation of clinical negligence costs have been made since the formation of the first wave of trusts in 1991. In the first four years the costs were limited to 0.5 per cent of turnover, leading potentially to an understatement of costs, at least compared with that required following SSAP 18. Later years have witnessed a more rigorous application of the accruals concept, although this has been complicated by the transfer of the financial risk of higher claims under the CNST and ELS schemes. Only in the last two years has there been a requirement to link the accounting disclosures to NHSLA returns.

The most recent guidance from the NHSE is aimed at achieving greater consistency across the NHS in both the allocation of these liabilities between NHS bodies and their valuation. The degree to which accruals-based accounting is successful in providing an accurate indication of a trust's exposure to future costs will depend critically on the resolution of ambiguities within the accounting guidelines.

2

Research Method

2.1 Introduction

The data for this study were collected in three stages using a variety of methods. The intention of the project team was to obtain both qualitative and quantitative evidence to meet the research objectives.

The project arose from an invitation by the director of corporate affairs at a general hospital NHS trust to review management and financial procedures relating to clinical negligence claims. Our initial meeting with the director and the trust's claims manager was held in September 1997, at which we expressed a desire to extend the study to include public and employers' liability claim procedures. We thought that the project had the potential for its research findings to be put in the public domain by extending the work to other trusts. At this stage the Research Foundation of CIMA was approached and agreed to provide funding to support the project.

2.2 Stage 1: Procedure and documentation review at an NHS hospital

The objectives of this first stage were to provide us with an understanding of the approach to claims and risk management in dealing with clinical negligence, public and employers' liability claims, and to introduce the team to relevant documentation. Between February and June 1998 we held a series of meetings and interviews with senior managers involved in risk management, claims handling, accounting and finance. The primary purpose here was to understand the processes, procedures and roles of the various trust personnel involved from the initial receipt or indication of a claim until the associated financial costs appeared in the accounts. Most of these interviews were tape-recorded and detailed notes were taken of those that were not. The tapes were transcribed in full for reasons of accuracy in recall of the detailed information provided in these meetings. We were also keen to identify those topics and themes that should be pursued in the later stages of the study.

Our work included the review of specimen sets of claimant files. These were intended to provide a cross-section of claim types rather than to be a representative sample. A total of sixteen categories was identified representing ELS, CNST, and employers' and public liability claims, and distinguishing between those claims which had been closed and those still open as well as those that were above and below excess levels for insurance or NHSLA purposes. The only category for which we were unable to find an example was a closed, CNST, above-excess claim. Reviewing these files proved to be useful in bringing to our attention unanticipated issues, such as the use of assessors for insurance claims, as well as providing documentary evidence of those procedures described in the earlier meetings. In view of the confidential nature of these files they were not taken off trust premises and details are not provided in this report.

Claims and risk management procedures were in a state of flux at this time. The trust was aiming to formalise its risk assessment processes and had circulated proposals for consideration by all directorates and departments. The existing claims manager was promoted to a new role as risk management co-ordinator, and a new complaints and risk manager was assigned during the period of our visit. It was also intended to reassign other roles in the department. A division of work between complaints and claims procedures had appeared to be maintained quite rigidly between three staff members up to this time. This was about to be changed, with the complaints and litigation (claims) officers combining their duties. There were also discussions about the continued use of their long-standing legal advisers. The trust was using two firms of solicitors and were considering placing all their clinical claims work into the hands of one of these firms. A new database for recording and managing clinical negligence claims was installed in the summer of 1998, but was not functioning fully at the time of our visit.

A key informant during this stage was the management accountant at the trust. He was a member of a regional committee that had been reviewing the recovery by trusts of their clinical negligence provisions. He referred us to NHSE guidance (NHSE, 1996b), which identifies four options for the recovery of provisions in prices. He then went on to explain that there were two further options not listed in the FDL, that is *(a)* not to charge it in prices at all, or *(b)* hope to recover it as part of additional cost pressures. For example:

> Suppose I set aside a provision in the year of £250,000, which bring up [total] provisions to £800,000. Our health authority says, 'OK, you get half of that.' That is it – it goes into the pot ... [so] our ability to hit our rate of return is one of those factors that we need to consider when we are setting provisions.

This type of explanation helped us to understand some of the options of managing and accounting for claims, which we used to support the interviews and questionnaire in the later stages of the project.

2.3 Stage 2: Interviews with managers

This stage of the project extended the exploration of process to a larger number of hospital trusts. We wished to obtain comparative evidence of systems of accounting in other trusts, including those in other regions. From our detailed study in Stage 1 we had concluded that our key informants in other trusts were likely to be:

- the director of finance, as he or she would have overall responsibility for accounting systems and financial performance and would be able to describe the discussions held at board level in respect of these risks;

- the management accountant, as he or she would be responsible for ensuring that costs and provisions were budgeted and reported within the trust and would be likely to deal with the financial implications of individual claims; and
- the claims manager, as he or she would be responsible for ensuring that claims were recorded and processed and would be likely to be the person dealing with the trust's legal advisers.

It was recognised that functional responsibility and job titles would not necessarily conform to this rigid typography. The claims management role in particular is sometimes undertaken along with other duties.

The selection of trusts for this second stage was carried out by, first, identifying six NHS regions in England and, second, by writing to eight trusts in each of the six regions asking for their help in the project.

We wished to interview trust managers in a number of regions in order to identify whether or not there were specific features within a region, or policies recommended by a regional office, that would affect trust procedures. The selection of the six NHS regions was made largely by measure of convenience. We wished to locate trusts that were within one day's travelling distance of Nottingham in order to avoid excessive travelling costs and overnight expenses. In practice, this meant that we omitted South Thames and the South and West regions.

We used the *Fitzhugh Directory of NHS Trusts* (HCIS, 1997) to provide rankings of the level of clinical negligence provisions and contingencies. Our study was limited to hospital-based trusts so we used Activity Group 2 (General Acute Units) from the *Fitzhugh Directory* for this selection. We decided to include trusts with both high and low reported values for provisions and contingencies in our selection. We reasoned that trust procedures (and the views of their managers) might differ, depending upon the value of claims against each trust and the extent to which the trust had decided to make provision for future liabilities. Using the *Fitzhugh Directory* listings we identified, in each region, two hospitals above and below the median value of clinical negligence provisions. A similar procedure was adopted in respect of contingent liabilities.

This gave us a selection of 48 trusts, each of which was sent a letter requesting assistance on the project (Appendix 1). We recognised that the confidential nature of the liability claims and the workload faced by many NHS finance directors would be likely to limit the response to our letter. We received fifteen positive replies, of which twelve were able to allow us access within the timeframe allowed in the project timetable. We were satisfied that this number would be sufficient to identify most of the issues of importance from the perspective of the managers to be interviewed, and that these twelve trusts represented a reasonable distribution of those factors we had used to determine the original selection.

Table 2.1 **Trusts visited for interviews.**

Trust	*Region*	*Provision*	*Contingency*
1	A	High	High
2	A	High	Low
3	B	Low	Low
4	C	High	High
5	C	High	Low
6	C	Low	Low
7	D	Low	High
8	D	Low	High
9	D	Low	High
10	E	Low	High
11	E	Low	High
12	F	High	Low

We completed a total of 34 interviews between August and October 1998. Interview guides (Appendices 2, 3 and 4) were used to ensure that key questions were asked, and each of these semi-structured interviews was tape-recorded. Wherever possible, at least two members of the research team attended the interviews so that there would be confirmation of the nature of the discussion that took place in addition to relying upon the recorded conversations. An attempt was made to arrange all three interviews at each trust on the same day, although this was not always possible because of prior commitments of the managers. Tapes were transcribed in full and copies of the transcripts were provided for all members of the team. The transcripts were used to identify differences to form the basis of a questionnaire suitable for distribution to all hospital trusts in England. Extracts from interviews are also included in the research findings section of this report.

2.4 Stage 3: Questionnaire design, distribution and analysis

The objective of this stage of the project was to provide a source of evidence of accounting procedures relating to claims which would be much wider than the detailed analysis of documentation in Stage 1 and the analysis of the interview transcripts from Stage 2. The *Fitzhugh Directory of NHS Trusts,* 6th edition (HCIS, 1998) was used to provide a listing of trusts extant in England at 31 March 1998. The *Directory* classifies trusts into six categories. Three of these categories (multiple activity, general acute units and specialist hospitals) were chosen as those to be circulated by questionnaire. This was consistent with the work in the first two stages. It recognised that claims procedures in the rest of the UK were different from those in England, and that clinical negligence claims were likely to be perceived as a more significant source of risk in hospital than community care, mental health service and ambulance trusts.

A first draft of the questionnaire, produced in November 1998, was continuously modified over the following month. We wanted to produce a questionnaire that would be sufficiently comprehensive to deal with all the major issues identified earlier in the project, but which would allow most questions to be answered by choosing an appropriate selection from a list. It was thought that this style of questionnaire would both encourage a higher participation rate than one needing longer, narrative responses, and enable a more robust quantitative analysis.

A pilot version of the questionnaire was sent to the hospitals that had been visited at Stage 2, with a letter asking them to comment on its suitability (Appendix 5). Two members of the project team visited one of these trusts to talk through the questionnaire with members of the accounting staff, and useful comments were received from a number of our earlier respondents. As a result, some further textual amendments were made to the questionnaire. One important amendment to the general design of the questionnaire was also made. The draft questionnaire had asked trusts to provide information in respect of the year ended 31 March 1998, as this was the last completed financial year for which data was available. However, several trusts pointed out that their procedures had changed in the last year and that it would be difficult and potentially confusing for trusts to refer back to the previous year when the current financial year would shortly be at an end. They recommended that the questionnaire refer to the year ended 31 March 1999 so that trusts could reply in respect of their most recent procedures and results.

We considered that this approach would help the questionnaire to be completed more easily and provide a more up-to-date analysis. However, this meant that the questionnaire needed to be issued around mid-March 1999. This would cause delay to completion of the project under our original timetable. It was at this time that an application was made to CIMA to defer production of this report until the end of May 1999.

The full questionnaire is reproduced in Appendix 6 and its accompanying letter in Appendix 7. The questionnaire was divided into eight sections dealing with the following issues:

A the management and administrative structures of the trust;
B the recording of likelihood of liability and quantum of claims;
C the determination of total provisions and contingencies;
D the extent to which claim costs are included in budgets;
E the extent to which claim costs are allocated in management accounts;
F the recovery of claim costs through prices;
G insurance arrangements; and
H the number of claims.

A total of 221 copies of the questionnaire were issued. A second copy, along with a reminder letter (Appendix 8), was sent to non-responders approximately four weeks later. Responses were eventually received from 64 trusts, representing a 29 per cent response rate.

In order to explore whether the sample of trusts which responded to our questionnaire was representative of the population of trusts contacted, we constructed some comparative tables in relation to trusts' characteristics (Appendix 9). These show that our respondents were drawn from the whole country, although slightly over-represented in the North and North-West, and slightly under-represented in London and the South-West. However, there were only small differences between the sample and population proportions by type and by wave, and the average size of trusts (as measured by total asset value) was very similar. As far as clinical negligence aggregates were concerned, our trusts reported slightly lower average gross provisions in 1998 (£2.3 million as opposed to £2.4 million for the population) and rather higher gross contingencies (£3.3 million as opposed to £2.4 million). Taking all these figures into account, we believe that we have a broadly representative cross-section of trusts in our sample, and that our findings can be interpreted accordingly.

3

Research Findings

3.1 Management and administrative structures

Walshe and Dineen (1998) report from a survey carried out that year that 99 per cent of trusts have a named member of the board who took responsibility for clinical risk management. This was usually the medical director or the nursing director, and in only 3 per cent of trusts was the director of finance that individual. Our objective was to identify what role, if any, the finance department took in issues relating to these claims.

Our interviews[1] suggested that directors of finance took a secondary, but nevertheless important, role in providing an indication of the likely financial consequences of these risks. In most cases trust boards did not appear to take a pro-active role in demanding such information, and the impression given was that most trust boards left the issue with the finance director, through a subcommittee structure to report the impact of these claims when necessary.

> The board is asking usually for quarterly reports from the claims manager about the sorts of claims and complaints coming through. It's my intention to do, probably twice a year, a full analysis of all the outstanding claims with the solicitors so that the board can see the extent of it. I have to say that they've probably not initiated the discussions a lot, yet, but when you prompt them obviously they are picking the issue up and they understand the worries. *(DF 8)*

Evidence from the survey revealed that finance departments in the majority of trusts are represented on committees concerned with both clinical and non-clinical risk management issues (Table A1). A corollary of this, of course, is that there appears to be a substantial minority of trusts where risk management issues are discussed without any direct involvement of the finance department.

Table A1. Is the director of finance (or another representative of the accounting/finance department) a member of the following trust committees?

1 In this section of the report, each trust at which interviews were held is identified by a number from 1 to 12, while quotations from individuals are indicated as either the director of finance (DF), management accountant (MA) or claims manager (CM). This description is used to represent the nature of the responsibilities of each interviewee and does not necessarily correspond to their formal job title.

Committee	*Finance member*
Clinical risk management	35
Clinical audit	11
Non-clinical risk	41
Health and safety	22

The absence of a financial representative from a committee does not necessarily mean that financial issues are not considered in that forum.

> Clearly there is a control issue and clearly all control issues have got financial consequences, but that doesn't mean that somebody from finance has to be sitting on every single committee in the organisation. Part of the role of my staff is, is to train and enable people so that the financial consequences of these decisions, contingencies or whatever are automatically thought about. It doesn't need somebody on the front line. *(DF 8)*

A majority of trusts included in the interviews had changed either their committee structure below board level or the reporting procedures relating to claims within the previous year.

> This is the first financial year we've actually tried to report to the audit committee the potential for clinical negligence. When they received the first schedule, which we put to them in April as independent directors, they were absolutely staggered at the potential liability. [The difficulty is that] anything from obstetrics you immediately put £1 million in because you just do not know what the complaint is and what the details will ultimately be. *(DF 6)*

> We had a risk management committee, which was a subcommittee of the board, and which technically is still in place but has not met for a year. We've now set up a different structure. We've underpinned the [committee] with a group that is basically working on the CNST standards. It's chaired by the director of nursing. There's a representative from each of the clinical directorates, their business manager and a nurse manager. There's somebody from medical records, clinical audit and myself for complaints and litigation. [At] the next board meeting, the chief executive is presenting a new committee structure for the trust which sorts out the corporate governance and clinical governance work. *(CM 5)*

We also asked in our survey which individual or department is principally responsible for the handling of claims. The results show that trusts adopt a wide range of job descriptions for those responsible. For clinical negligence, there were three broad groupings which stood out from the others: nine trusts mentioned risk managers or a close equivalent; nine mentioned legal services, litigation departments or an equivalent; six referred to claims or complaints managers; the remainder were varied, ranging from nursing services, through the finance department to human resources. Clearly, there is a wide diversity of roles allocated here:

> I am responsible for collating the league table information. I am now charged with looking at the new NHS framework and what that is going to mean in terms of monitoring for us in the future. Because of a previous life I also have a hat on that says I provide the trust with advice on the Mental Health Act. I am the complaints manager under the NHS complaints procedure and since April of this year ... I am also responsible for handling the legal issues in relation to medico-legal cases. I am also on the clinical risk management committee. I report to the chief executive. *(CM 6)*

> I do think that the tie-in with complaints is extremely important. Not only from dealing with the complaints but dealing with staff as well. I am finding ... that patients are testing the water by complaining first, and so I tend to get very involved in complaints and know it from start to finish because I have to draft the final report and so I know exactly what's gone on. Now when they go on to litigation I then know that case, inside out. *(CM 8)*

3.2 Estimating the likelihood of liability and quantum

It was clear from our interviews that the description of likelihood of liability used by trusts did vary and was most commonly influenced by descriptions provided by trust solicitors. Some trusts had used descriptions representing probability but without assigning a particular quantitative value (using terms such as 'low, medium or high risk'). Probability is often described in percentage terms and in a manner that conforms to categories given in the *NHS Trust Manual of Accounts.*

Our survey revealed considerable variation between trusts in the way in which information was recorded internally on the likelihood of liability of claims.

Table B1. How does the finance department (or claims management department) record information on the *likelihood of liability* for a particular claim?

Please tick one box in each column	***Clinical negligence***	***Employers' liability***	***Public liability***
As a percentage probability of liability (e.g. 0–5%, 5–50%, 50%–95%)	27	19	19
As a category representing probability of liability (e.g. low, medium, high)	24	24	24
Both	13	7	7
Neither – different system used	0	10	10

For clinical negligence, those trusts using a percentage method of recording liability estimates exceeded those using categorical methods, whereas the opposite applied for employers' and public liability claims. In any case, it was clear from the responses to question B2 that trusts were usually capable of making a direct mapping from the categorical headings to the percentages given in FDL(97)13/(NHSE, 1997). Whichever classification was used, it did not always remove the subjectivity which trusts had to apply in determining their provisions and contingent liabilities. One particular issue was the tendency of solicitors to define probability as exactly 50 per cent or 'medium risk' for many claims:

> Probability is low, medium, high ... it will generally be medium unless it is quite clearly rubbish, in which case it is low, or we've got an open admission from the consultant that we screwed up, in which case it is high. *(CM 3)*

Although trusts may be provided with likelihood probabilities that coincide with those given in FDL(97)13, this does not necessarily mean that provisions are made on a consistent basis between trusts. For example, there remains open the question as to whether any claim which is assigned a probability of payment likelihood of exactly 50 per cent should be provided in full, or partially or not at all. This can have a considerable effect on the quantum of the provision.

> We use the most likely [settlement value] to produce all our accounting estimates. They [solicitors] also attach a percentage probability of [claimant] success to it. So if it is above 50 per cent probability of success then we provide for the full amount of the potential claim. If it is less than 50 per cent then we provide for nothing. If it's actually on the 50 per cent line then we provide for half of it. We thought that was a simple way of dealing with it. I know the region are planning to try and get rid of everything that falls on the exactly 50 per cent line so that it is above or below. *(MA 8)*

It was apparent that there was considerable variation in the determination of which classifications of claims to include, wholly or partially, in the provision.

> Well, the solicitors told us that there was a 50 per cent chance, so we said that anything that was 50.1 per cent we would accrue for. *(DF 7)*

> The problem was that the solicitors estimate ... 90 per cent of them as medium. Which gives you a difficult job then when you get to year-end ... so we have to come up with a basis on which to estimate them. It's about 25 per cent. *(DF 3)*

> The auditors have accepted the provisions that we've provided.... They think it's sufficiently prudent at this stage ... we provide for 100 per cent high, 50 per cent medium and this year zero for low, in previous years it was 25 per cent for low. *(DF 4)*

This ambiguity was captured in our survey, in which over a quarter of all trusts indicated uncertainty over whether they would make a provision for a claim where they believed there was a 50 per cent chance of liability (Table B2). In one response it was explicitly stated that 'the Trust would make a realistic estimate of cases at 50 per cent probability'. For claims rated at less than 50 per cent liability, most (but not all) trusts indicated that they would definitely *not* provide. For claims rated at greater than 50 per cent liability, the converse was true. Clearly, there is a wide distribution of policies, ranging from those who feel it is necessary and prudent to make at least a part provision, even for those claims which are unlikely to require payment, to those who make a judgement on provision based on other factors, even for those claims which are likely to require payment at some time.

Table B2. What action is taken in the light of information on the likelihood of liability when deciding whether to make a gross *provision* (i.e. before recovery from CNST/ELS or other insurers) for an individual claim in the trust's financial accounts?

	Action		
Percentage likelihood of trust liability	***Definitely provide***	***Definitely do not provide***	***May provide***
0%	0	52	3
Over 0% but under 50%	6	43	8
50%	35	6	16
Over 50% but under 95%	48	1	8
95% and over	56	1	1

It also became apparent during interviews that trusts were prepared to omit liabilities from the provision on the grounds that the quantum could not be assessed with reasonable accuracy. The failure to provide for such liabilities would appear to be consistent with SSAP 18, which requires provision to be made only when payment is probable and can be assessed with reasonable accuracy. This requirement is adopted in the various editions of the *NHS Trust Manual of Accounts*.

> We had very strong debates a year ago with district audit, saying, 'Look, we know we are going to be liable but, at this stage in the claim, we cannot determine the amount with reasonable accuracy. Therefore, following the definition in the *Manual of Accounts*, we are not accruing. We are showing it as a note to the accounts as a contingent liability.' They then argued that we were not showing a prudent approach.
>
> We are only in a position to determine with reasonable accuracy when we have notification from ... our solicitors. If they say, 'We think you are going to be liable for £50,000,' well, that's reasonable accuracy. If it's just, 'We think you are going to be liable but really at this stage we haven't got any indication in terms of how much,' that is not with reasonable accuracy. *(DF 10)*

Once a decision has been made on provision in relation to a particular claim, a second-order decision is required over whether to disclose as a contingent liability any claim (or part of a claim) which has not been provided for. Table B3 shows the results on this from our survey. Here the dispersion of policies is even wider than in Table B2, leading to some possible inconsistencies. First, where a claim is expected *never* to be paid (probability of liability 0 per cent), nineteen trusts said that they would still disclose the amount as a contingent liability. Second, of the 56 trusts which said they would definitely provide for claims assessed at over 95 per cent liability, fifteen also said that they would definitely include these as a contingent liability. These responses are consistent only if the claim was somehow divided up and each element reported separately.

Table B3. What action is taken in the light of information on the likelihood of liability when deciding whether to include part or all of an individual claim as a gross *contingent liability* (i.e. before recovery from CNST/ELS or other insurers) in the trust's financial accounts?

	Action		
Percentage likelihood of trust liability	*Definitely include as a contingent liability*	*Definitely do not include as a contingent liability*	*May include as a contingent liability*
0%	25	29	1
Over 0% but under 50%	43	9	5
50%	17	20	12
Over 50% but under 95%	15	29	6
95% and over	15	33	3

The inclusion, within contingencies, of cases with an apparent 0 per cent likelihood of payment is strictly required from the *NHS Trust Manual of Accounts*. Such an approach is illogical in the extreme: if the payment probability is really 0 per cent then payment will never be made. If the probability of payment is more than zero, but is very low, the contingent liability might be considered to be remote and, following SSAP 18, would not be disclosed.

> For contingencies, we use the highest possible amount.... If there is an amount assessed against the case but the probability was zero, we'd still put that in as a contingent liability. *(MA 7)*

It is also apparent, from Table B3, that some trusts may include, within contingent liabilities, some of the estimated costs of cases where the likelihood of payment is expected to be more than 50 per cent. This may be explained by those trusts which provide for that part of the claim based upon the likelihood of payment and include in contingent liabilities the remaining part of the claim based upon 100 per cent less the likelihood of payment. This is consistent with the use of an expected-value method of determining provisions. Another way to explain the use of contingencies for these cases is that trusts base the amount of their provision on the most likely estimate and include the difference between the worst-case outcome and the most likely estimate within contingencies. One of the trust managers, in interview, explained it this way:

> The auditors have told us that we are understating our contingencies. We were taking our contingency as only the ones that fell below the 50 per cent. Those that you were likely to pay out, you've got a possible payout and a realistic payout. We were taking the realistic payout [for the provision] and they said that the difference between the realistic payout and the possible payout should go into the contingency as well. *(MA 2)*

Irrespective of whether a claim is reported as a provision or a contingent liability, some estimate is needed of the amount the trust would have to pay out if the claim were successful. Given the uncertainty over the outcome of litigation, trusts, with or without external legal advice, may choose to record a range of estimates.

Table B4. How does the finance department (or claims management department) record information on the estimated quantum (i.e. gross claims payable) and legal or associated costs for a particular claim?

Tick all boxes that apply	*Quantum*	*Trust's legal costs*	*Claimant's legal costs*
Best-case estimate (minimum gross loss to trust)	4	1	1
Worst-case estimate (maximum gross loss to trust)	19	10	12
Most likely estimate	51	47	46
No estimate recorded	0	2	1

The responses indicate that the most likely estimate (i.e. the mean of the subjective distribution) is most often available, with a significant minority of trusts also having available a more prudent worst-case estimate.

We were interested to discover whether trusts combined their beliefs about liability and quantum when making a provision in the accounts. That is, did they make an estimate of the expected payment (probability of liability times most likely quantum) when calculating the size of the provision for a given claim?

Table B5. Which of these estimates of quantum is used when estimating the amount to be included as a gross *provision* (i.e. before recovery from CNST/ELS or other insurers) for a particular claim in the trust's financial accounts?

	Unweighted	*Weighted by likelihood of liability*
Best-case estimate	1	0
Worst-case estimate	5	6
Most likely estimate	35	15
None of the above	1	1

Five trusts declared the most prudent approach of using a worst-case estimate without discounting for the likelihood of liability. The majority of trusts simply use the most likely estimate of quantum without weighting for liability (in itself a relatively prudent approach).

Contingent liabilities, by their nature, are estimates of the liabilities which will probably not materialise, but which are reported to provide an indication of potential liabilities facing the trust. Consequently, a higher proportion of trusts reported the use of worst-case estimates when estimating the amount to disclose (Table B6). A substantial number of trusts also reported that they would not make a deduction for any provision made on the same claim, which could lead to double counting in any attempt to calculate the aggregate liabilities of the trust.

Table B6. Which of these estimates of quantum is used when estimating the amount to be included as a gross *contingent liability* (i.e. before recovery from CNST/ELS or other insurers) for a particular claim in the note to the trust's financial accounts?

	With a deduction for the provision	*Without a deduction for the provision*
Best-case estimate	3	0
Worst-case estimate	11	5
Most likely estimate	26	14
None of the above (please explain)	4	1

The results of this part of the survey indicate considerable diversity in how trusts go about estimating the likelihood of liability and quantum of individual claims. There is variation in the way in which likelihood of liability is recorded, and the action taken to determine whether claims will be included within provisions or contingent liabilities. The calculation of the amount provided for each claim also varies depending upon whether trusts use worst-case or most likely estimate, and whether or not the quantum of a claim is weighted by likelihood of liability.

3.3 Determining accounting provisions and contingencies

Once trusts have decided for each particular claim whether it should be provided for or disclosed, and for how much, they then face the second-order problem of determining what should be the overall total of provisions and contingent liabilities reported in the relevant year. This involves, first, deciding whether to deduct from the aggregate an amount reflecting the anticipated recovery from third parties such as insurers or the CNST; and second, whether the resulting aggregate should be adjusted in some way to reflect wider considerations. Table C1 shows that the majority of trusts assume complete recovery for both provisions and contingent liabilities.

Table C1. What assumptions are made about any recoveries* under relevant insurance contracts in computing the *net* provisions and contingent liabilities in the trust's financial accounts? Please tick one box in each column.

* Recovery means recovery from insurers in line with the terms and conditions of the contract, taking into account any excesses or deductibles.

Net provisions	***Clinical negligence***	***Employers' liability***	***Public liability***
Complete recovery assumed	53	50	51
No recovery assumed	3	6	6
Other	5	3	2

Net contingencies	***Clinical negligence***	***Employers' liability***	***Public liability***
Complete recovery assumed	50	46	46
No recovery assumed	5	6	6
Other	3	3	3

Tables C2 and C3 show that a minority of trusts adjust the aggregate of provisions, making reference to 'prudence' and 'realism' as a justification for doing so.

Table C2. Is the trust's net aggregate provision equal to the sum of the net provisions on individual cases, or is this sum adjusted before inclusion in the financial accounts? Please tick one box.

Sum included without further adjustment	53
Sum included after further adjustment – upwards	7
Sum included after further adjustment – downwards	3

Table C3. If an adjustment is made to obtain the net provision, what factors influence this adjustment? Tick any box that applies.

Requirement to achieve break-even on income and expenditure	0
Requirement to meet EFL target	0
Requirement of 6 per cent return on net assets	1
Need to be prudent in estimating provisions	4
Need to be realistic in estimating provisions	4
Pressure from purchasers/commissioners	0
Pressure from members of trust board	0
Pressure from trust's audit committee	0
Pressure from trust's external auditors	1

The requirement for provisions to be consistent with CNST returns implies that its quantum should be based upon specific cases on file. However, we did come across one trust that had included a general element as part of its provision. This may be interpreted as overproviding for liabilities if the individual cases have been assessed with care, based upon all information available at the time that the accounts were prepared.

> [The auditors] have been inundated with a number of technical releases and loads of advice which all tends to point to the audit trail for the provision being clear and precise in terms of named claims quantified by your legal adviser and leading to the provision. So they were, shall we say, uncertain about the rightness of having a general provision? In the end it's less than £50,000 and the view was it wasn't material, so in the end they didn't dispute or ask us to remove that provision. *(MA 3)*

A number of other trusts indicated that they had made adjustments to reduce their provision in the light of comparisons between payments made and previous estimates. For example:

> This year we did an exercise which looked at what the actual level of claim was against the contingency figures that [our solicitors] advised.... We found that we had a 13 per cent reduction in the value that we are paying out. We want to apply that percentage reduction this year to the value of all of our liabilities. The auditors said ... that they wanted us to produce some records that list every case separately and did an assessment of every one. In the end ... using this mechanism I take a figure that we've put in the annual accounts and then, in effect, I work backwards from that by trying to work out what the actual reduction was on each case. *(MA 8)*

> We've got the figures now for eleven hospitals ... it's so constant this figure, it's absolutely amazing, 66 per cent, exactly two-thirds of cases that come in, letters before action, they will never ever do anything. Basically what will happen is, you will disclose the notes then you won't hear from the other side. [In] 15 per cent of cases we find we need to get further expert evidence, I think about half of those will probably settle halfway through and 17 per cent to 19 per cent of cases we settle. These figures are pretty constant now, over two and a half years. They are all on database and we check the figures every six months and they are pretty constant. *(CM 11)*

Very few trusts reported that they adjust the aggregate of contingent liabilities, as shown in Tables C4 and C5 below:

Table C4. Is the net contingent liability equal to the sum of the individual cases or is this sum adjusted before inclusion in the financial accounts? Please tick one box.

Sum included without further adjustment	58
Sum included after further adjustment – upwards	1
Sum included after further adjustment – downwards	1

Table C5. If such an adjustment is made to obtain the net contingent liability, what factors influence this adjustment? Tick any box that applies.

Need to be prudent in estimating contingent liabilities	1
Need to be realistic in estimating contingent liabilities	2
Pressure from purchasers/commissioners	0
Pressure from members of trust board	0
Pressure from trust's audit committee	0
Pressure from trust's external auditors	0
Other (please explain)	0

The fact that relatively few trusts adjust the aggregate of individual provisions and contingent liabilities when drawing up their accounts puts greater emphasis on the decisions made in relation to particular claims, which, as we have seen above, can vary considerably.

Finally, in this section of the questionnaire, we asked whether any explicit figure is included in the aggregate provisions or contingent liabilities for potential claims that have not yet been notified to the trust. No trust in the survey reported that any such value was included in their provision. It would appear that the value of the 'incurred but not reported' (IBNR) claims of trusts is not readily available at individual trust level. This suggests that the requirement in HSC 1999/174 (Annex C, para. 4) (NHSE, 1999c) that all NHS bodies should work towards identifying the value of their IBNR cases will be problematic, at least in the short term. It seems unlikely that many trusts will be in a position to provide a reliable estimate to make a provision for their IBNR claims when FRS 12 is first applied in their 1999/2000 financial statements. It is also interesting to note that, while the NHS accounts do not currently include a provision for IBNR claims, the NAO figure of £2.8 billion (mentioned on p.1 of this report) does include £1 billion for IBNR claims. This suggests that the NAO's figure is not constructed from estimates provided by individual NHS bodies.

3.4 Treatment in NHS trusts' budgets

In addition to finding out how trusts reported their clinical negligence, employers' liability and public liability claims in their accounts, we were also interested in how the costs arising from these claims were budgeted for. Table D1 shows how the trusts responded to our question about the budgeting of CNST contributions and insurance premiums. We were particularly concerned to see whether premiums were allocated to specific clinical directorates or service activities:

> We are not going to devolve a bigger insurance charge down to obstetrics. You could reflect it in your obstetrics pricing, say, if you wanted to, but you wouldn't charge it into their budget ... there's no way they can manage that without making mincemeat and nonsense of their budget. To put the thing into context I think the amount we paid out last year was not a lot, ... it's less than one-tenth of 1 per cent [of the trust budget]. I'm wrestling this year with £10.5m worth of cost pressure and you know, it's just one of those things you take on the chin and find some saving elsewhere to fund it. That's the way I look at it. *(DF 12)*

In fact, Table D1 shows complete unanimity in relation to the treatment of premiums: in all trusts, they are included in budgets as central overheads and not allocated to particular clinical directorates. Presumably the difficulty in dividing a premium which is set globally for the trust as a whole is the explanation for this commonality of practice.

Table D1. How are the *insurance premiums* for clinical negligence, employers' and public liability incorporated in your trust's budgeting system?

	Clinical negligence	*Employers' liability*	*Public liability*
Premiums not included in budgets at any level	0	0	0
Premiums included in budgets as central overheads and not allocated to particular clinical directorates	61	63	63
Premiums included in the budgets of specific clinical directorates, but not allocated to specific service activities	0	0	0
Premiums included in the budgets as a direct cost of related service activity	0	0	0
Other methods of budgeting	0	0	0

When the same question is asked in relation to the uninsured losses (that is, the costs arising from the settlement of claims net of recoveries), a number of trusts surprisingly reported that they did not budget for these costs at all (Table D2). Of those that did budget, all but one did not allocate them to directorates, in spite of the fact that it would have been relatively easy to identify the source of liability for each claim. However, while the source of liability may be evident, the uncertainties surrounding the ultimate costs of each claim may deter allocation, at least while payments for claims remain at modest levels.

> I think it would be quite difficult to allocate [these costs] given the uncertainty about the levels of claims, the risks associated with coming to settle that and the funding issues. I think, as time goes on, trusts of this size will probably be looking at £1 million a year in premiums, claims and excesses, and legal costs, probably within the next three or four years. At that stage I think probably we need to take a different view of it. *(DF 8)*

Table D2. How is an allowance for *'uninsured' losses* arising from clinical negligence, employers' and public liability incorporated in your trust's budgeting system?

	Clinical negligence	*Employers' liability*	*Public liability*
Costs not included in budgets at any level	11	11	11
Costs included in budgets as central overheads and not allocated to particular clinical directorates	53	51	51
Costs included in the budgets of specific clinical directorates, but not allocated to specific service activities	0	2	2
Costs included in the budgets as a direct cost of related service activity	0	0	0
Other methods (please explain)	0	0	0

3.5 Allocation in NHS trusts' management accounts

The same degree of consistency was observed when we asked how trusts allocated their legal liabilities for management accounting purposes:

> It doesn't get reported to individual clinicians or directorates. It does get reported separately in the monthly accounts that we produce because ... we allocated a sum for interim payments that are going to be made through the year. We have a budget now and show the actuals. *(MA 4)*

Tables E1 and E2 show that both premiums and uninsured losses are almost universally treated as central overheads and not allocated to particular clinical directorates in the trusts' management accounts.

Table E1. How are the *insurance premiums* for clinical negligence, and employers' and public liability allocated in your trust's management accounting system?

	Clinical negligence	*Employers' liability*	*Public liability*
Premiums treated as central overheads and not allocated to particular clinical directorates	59	61	61
Premiums treated as overheads of specific clinical directorate to which claim relates, but not allocated to specific service activities	1	0	0
Premiums treated as a direct cost of service activity to which claim relates	0	0	0

Table E2. How are the *'uninsured' losses* for clinical negligence, and employers' and public liability allocated in your trust's management accounting system?

	Clinical negligence	*Employers' liability*	*Public liability*
Costs treated as central overheads and not allocated to particular clinical directorates	63	59	59
Costs treated as overheads to the specific clinical directorate to which claim relates, but not allocated to specific service activities	0	1	1
Costs treated as a direct cost of the service activity to which claim relates	0	2	2

The near unanimity of this treatment of costs as central overheads provides a sharp contrast with the intention, when the internal market was created in 1991, that these costs would be included in procedure prices. The expectation, at that time, was that prices charged to purchasers would reflect different levels of quality and provide an incentive to trusts to reduce risk. Our interviews with directors of finance suggest that such allocations are not made because:

- they are difficult to assess in terms of both quantum and responsibility;
- the payments (and sometimes provisions) have been relatively small to date; and
- allocation for pricing purposes is irrelevant as purchasers will not or cannot pay for these costs.

This last issue is considered further in the next section.

3.6 Recovery of costs in prices

Having established the various policies adopted by trusts to estimate and provide for the costs of clinical negligence and other liabilities, we were concerned to find out how they recovered these costs from their purchasers. From our interviews, it was clear that there was some resistance from purchasers to accepting insurance premiums or CNST contributions as a cost, but that various means were found to pass it on:

> It's hugely difficult to get the purchaser to accept any increased cost, and if we were to go to them and say our CNST premium has gone up because we are more risky they would say, 'Get your act together, reduce your risk, reduce your premium'.... So we hide it. But don't tell the purchaser that. *(DF 1)*

> What we have agreed [last year] with our authority is that it will fund on a recurrent basis, insurance premiums, including CNST, so that when we notify them of an increase in the insurance they actually include it as part of the baseline contract. *(DF 2)*

In relation to CNST contributions, Table F1 shows that eight trusts reported that purchasers refused to accept the cost, seven said that purchasers had agreed to make a specific cash settlement to cover the cost, and the remainder recovered the contribution through their overall prices, in some cases as an identified separate component. In relation to employers' liability and public liability insurance premiums, the picture was similar, although fewer trusts reported a negotiated cash payment from purchasers and more included the cost in their overall price structure.

Table F1. How is the trust's contribution to the CNST, and the insurance premiums paid to commercial insurers, recovered from purchasers?

	CNST	*Employers' liability*	*Public liability*
Purchasers do not accept this cost	8	8	8
Purchasers have agreed to make a specific cash settlement to cover this cost either in the year of accrual or at a later date	7	2	2
Cost is identified separately and included in overall price structure	10	5	5
Cost is included in the overall price structure although not identified separately	32	45	45

The picture in respect of the recovery of uninsured costs appears to be even more diverse than that of recovery of premiums. It became clear from interviews that some trusts had never been able to convince their health authorities to accept the costs of claims as an allowable element within prices.

> Our health authority won't accept it as a cost pressure. [They see it as] a trust issue and that's been the brick-wall approach. *(DF 5)*

However, there was expectation among many of those interviewed that some kind of structured agreement with purchasers would be able to be negotiated in the future. Such expectation was based upon new arrangements for the recovery of provisions and similar costs that were to be implemented from April 1998 (HSC, 1998/105) (NHSE, 1998a). This new NHS policy requires regular (typically quarterly) meetings between trusts and their commissioners to agree how the recovery of provisions should be reflected in their accounts. Trusts will then record as debtors that part of their provisions that are recoverable from their commissioners, with cash settlement taking place at the time of payment of the claim by the trust.

These new arrangements are intended to ensure that trusts and commissioners 'work together in an open and participative manner to agree the causes and values of NHS Trusts' provisions' (HSC, 1998/105, para. 11) (NHSE, 1998a). However, the scheme may still require considerable time and skill in negotiation, given the difficulty in allocating particular claims to particular purchasers:

> We have a difficulty here in that we have contracts with over 50 purchasers ... and obviously different purchasers want to do different systems. Up until now we've simply built this into prices, movements in the premium and expected movements in the accruals.
>
> Under the new system, we are, each quarter, telling [our host purchaser] of the details of the changes in the accrual and the district of residence of the patient. But they tried to slither out of it. They've already had a debate about whether they are responsible for all of them or they are just responsible for [local residents] or whether they are responsible for the proportion of the costs that relates to the [local residents'] share of our overall prices. So increasingly we are moving to the view that each health authority, instead of it being built into prices, will pay for the clinical negligence excess in respect of their patients.
>
> And this is the debate, purchasers still haven't [agreed to the scheme]. My view is that the guidance was wrong, in a trust like this anyway, with it moving to primary care groups where you've probably got 300 purchasers. We should simply build it into prices and manage the accrual in the cash flow ourselves, like any other trading organisation. That is not the view of our host purchaser. Distant purchasers are saying, 'Your host purchaser ought to be dealing with this,' and so we are faced with a whole load of confusion about the accounting for this and which option we go for. *(FD 12)*

Table F2 shows that a relatively large number of trusts have been unable to recover uninsured liability costs from purchasers at all, particularly in respect of employers' and public liability claims. For clinical negligence claims, where the purchaser is willing to meet the cost, the most common arrangement is for purchasers to agree to pay the net cost of claims as and when they are paid to claimants. For claims where the purchaser is willing to meet the cost, the most common arrangement is for the accrued cost to be included in the overall price structure, although not identified separately.

Table F2. How does the trust recover the *uninsured* costs of clinical negligence, employers' liability and public liability claims from purchasers?

	Clinical negligence	*Employers' liability*	*Public liability*
Purchasers have not accepted this cost	10	18	18
Purchasers make a cash settlement to cover the cost *in the year of accrual*	2	1	1
Purchasers have agreed to make a cash settlement to cover the cost *at a later date* (e.g. at the time of payment)	26	11	11
The *accrued* cost is identified separately and included in the overall price structure	2	2	2
The *expected settlement cost* for the coming period is identified separately and included in the overall price structure	3	2	2
The *accrued* cost is included in the overall price structure, although not identified separately	9	15	15
The *expected settlement cost* for the coming period is included in the overall price structure although not identified separately	4	7	7

It can be seen that there is considerable variability of responses in Table F2. In respect of clinical negligence costs, the variability is consistent with the options in NHSE (1996b) and the further methods of (non) recovery discussed with the management accountant in the first stage of the project. It also supports our discussions with trust directors of finance and management accountants during Stage 2. There appears to be a bimodal result in respect of the recovery of the uninsured element of employers' and public liability claims. Either the costs are included in the overall price structure, but not separately identified, or these costs are not recovered at all. These results may reflect the lower incidence or uninsured element of these claims.

3.7 Insurance arrangements

It was explained earlier that trusts may want to utilise the NHSLA and external insurers to gain benefits from risk transfer, risk distribution, risk financing, cost-effective advice, risk management incentives and investment income. Membership of a mutual risk pool or the purchase of insurance would be expected to reduce fluctuations in I&E charges and provisions. One immediate possibility is that the occurrence of unexpected liabilities would cause trusts to fail to meet the 6 per cent and break-even financial targets imposed by the NHS. However, failure to meet these targets for such a reason may not be a problem:

> My view is, increasingly, is it's a reasonable explanation of why you've not hit your financial target. If I say, 'Oh, three years ago we had a bit of a bad patch in the obstetric hospital and that's why we've not hit the financial target,' then ...

> I wouldn't wince too much about doing that. In some ways clinical negligence is still seen as excusable and in some cases a random act of God. *(DF 12)*

On the other hand, the political pressure on trust directors can be a powerful motivating factor. One of the directors of finance recalled the decision to join the CNST:

> We actually had quite a debate on whether we should be a member or not. At the end of the day it sort of went something like, 'I don't want to be the finance director in a trust that isn't a member, when it has a major clinical claim against it.' And therefore we became a member. *(DF 1)*

The pressure on senior management to avoid a worst-case scenario may be particularly intense.

> If this was something that the trust itself had made no provision for and it resulted in a major deficit at the year end, the first person [to be held to account] would be the chief executive. Now, if he was unable to give a satisfactory answer I think he, and probably the chairman, would find themselves so embarrassed, or pressure put upon them that they were not in control over their organisation, that their future [at the trust] is going to be extremely limited. That's the ultimate sanction, and that wouldn't just be the chief executive. You would find the director of finance would be going out the door at the same time because [the] director of finance has to know everything. So it is the scenario that, no matter what we do, as finance people, we will always be criticised because we didn't have something there, whether that might be a provision or process and procedures in place. I would think a director of finance would have to use something really substantial so as to avoid having an insurance premium to help them out. *(DF 6)*

When discussing the concept of risk distribution, many directors of finance and management accountants felt that all trusts with the same CNST risk management standard should pay the same rate of contribution. However, it is a fundamental principle of private insurance (in contrast to social insurance) that premiums or contributions should be related to an *ex ante* assessment of the risk. Failure to do this leaves the insurer or pool vulnerable to the operation of *adverse selection,* whereby members which know themselves to be high risk will try to overinvest in insurance whereas those which know themselves to be low risk will do the opposite. This appears to have been a problem in the early years of the CNST:

> It's not that we are risk averse, it was just so obvious we were going to end up saving that premium with the level of claims we could see were coming through ... the level of premium we have been paying is still less than one-half [of one] serious claim. So it is self-evident that it's going to pay for itself. *(DF 12)*

Furthermore, the problem of cherry-picking can arise in pools or insurance markets which are competitive as insurers attempt to pick off the low-risk members by offering them special deals or lower contribution rates. Low-risk trusts are likely to try to leave risk pools:

> They should be investing this money on the international markets and building up a nice fund. Now, instead, at the moment everyone is laughing because they [the CNST] are charging quite small premiums really. But what they don't realise, of course, is that the CNST haven't paid out a single penny yet.... What's going to happen when the first cerebral palsy claims come into town? So this year, maybe the next, you get about 5, 6, 7, 8, 9, 10, 20 cerebral palsy claims being settled; then suddenly the premiums will just go sky high. I'd say in a couple of years ... I'll probably recommend that we get out of CNST because I am not going to let this trust subsidise the negligence of other trusts around the country....
> My view is that CNST will not be able to exist in its present form. I think when the big premiums start coming in ... you will get a mass pull-out by a lot of trusts, unless the government steps in. *(CM 11)*

Interviews with directors of finance point to cash management, rather than accruals-based financial targets, as the main motive for the purchase of insurance:

> In theory, [the financial targets] should be of equal importance ... but nationally far more importance is placed on the NHS not spending more than its overall cash allocation, in our context the EFL. Therefore, that's more important and so we've never exceeded our EFL. *(DF 3)*

> The EFL is the most important target of the lot. But nobody's got any excuse for missing the EFL. If you can't manage your EFL you want shooting. *(DF 12)*

> The cash will be a bigger problem than I&E. If I went into a deficit because of this sort of thing I'd be fairly relaxed about it, to be honest – I wouldn't lose a lot of sleep – but I'd lose more sleep on managing the cash because if I don't have the cash then I can't pay the salaries and wages. *(DF 1)*

> We can't go bust, but somebody has to fund the claim from somewhere. So therefore you've got to create the means to give that cash back. I would find it difficult to tell doctors and physicians out there, 'Sorry folks, you've got to make £1 million savings this year to pay back this claim because we haven't insured ourselves.' They'll probably turn round and say, 'It was something you should have forecast and foreseen.' So you are caught between a rock and a hard place. So you have to make savings. Of course there is always one way ... and that's to completely abandon our capital scheme for a year. *(DF 6)*

Finance directors are also appreciative of the role of insurance in providing cost-effective advice:

> For me it spreads the liabilities across the NHS. You've got somebody who's actually got an overview of all the claims that are going through and if they see a lot of claims going through in a particular area or a particular field, they can notify people. It's actually about a sharing of knowledge and experience. *(DF 2)*

There was scepticism about the negative impact of the CNST and commercial insurance on risk management incentives (and the need to correct for this problem via the introduction of partial risk sharing). Some argued that it is simple good business sense to control the adverse impact of risk on patients and employees:

> I don't discuss with colleagues the level of insurance and say, 'It's all right, we've got nil excess – you can let everybody go and damage their backs.' Because we all know it will get reflected back in premiums and loss of excess [and] if we are keeping vigilant on health and safety risks, that's for the benefit of our staff and we want to be a good employer. *(DF 11)*

However, there was evidently some mixed experience of the value of insurance discounts and excesses in rewarding and motivating risk management. Some trusts were anticipating substantial discounts in their premiums and CNST contributions:

> I see [the CNST] more as a pooling arrangement ... where achieving the different levels of attainment on risk management will count for more and more. Contributions that we are making on an annual basis will obviously be rather more significant [in the future] and therefore the ability to rebate those or discount them by achieving higher levels of risk management standard will be very much more meaningful. *(DF 9)*

> [The CNST] is a general sort of mutual fund as far as I am concerned. In the long term you expect to recover back what you paid in. You are not expected to gain or lose. It's a way of smoothing, essentially, I think that's what it was intended to do and ... I don't feel there is a great deal of evidence to suggest that it's any different. The mechanism for rewarding the good and the gracious, like ourselves, is the fact that there is discounting of the premium. If we start paying at the £1 to £2 million a year premium rates then the 25 per cent that I expect to be getting for discount, if we are the top dogs, is going to be a lot of money worth saving. *(DF 11)*

On the other hand, other trusts had a mixed experience in obtaining such discounts from commercial insurers:

> Employers' liability and public liability, we cover through commercial insurance. Those commercial insurers we work with have given a reduced price for

demonstrating that we have proper procedures and policies in place for managing public liability and employers' liability. I remember when I used to work here, way back ... there was a huge amount of work done by the planning directorate on non-clinical risk and getting ourselves in shape so that we got the best insurance deal and managing the claims process properly. *(DF 12)*

We looked at renewing our insurance and we didn't think we were getting a good deal because we felt that we had put a lot of effort into managing risk and we were reasonably successful. What emerged was everybody renews their insurance in April [so] they don't really have time to make a thorough assessment because they are trying to assess so many ... so we thought we'd change our assessment date to November. *(CM 3)*

Looking at the total cost of liability risk to trusts, it is conventional to measure this as the sum of premium contributions and the uninsured losses that result from risk retention. In this section we attempt to quantify the former and to assess what proportion of the overall risk is retained by each trust. Tables G1 to G3a summarise our findings in relation to the premiums paid out on average by our survey respondents over the last two financial years.

Table G1. Is the trust a member of the Clinical Negligence Scheme for Trusts? *Yes:* 48

	1997/98	*1998/99*
Annual mean contribution £	46,480	70,233

Table G2. Is the trust insured against employers' liability claims? *Yes:* 20

	1997/98	*1998/99*
Annual mean premium £	57,120	52,901

Table G3. Is the trust insured against public liability claims? *Yes:* 20

	1997/98	*1998/99*
Annual mean premium £	18,612	28,482

Table G3a. Is the trust insured against EL/public liability claims combined? *Yes:* 28

	1997/98	*1998/99*
Annual mean premium £	58,546	60,888

Table G1 shows that the average contribution to CNST is increasing rapidly, whereas the other tables show smaller changes for employers' and public liability insurance premiums. The former reflects the nature of the CNST as a mutual, non-funded scheme whose contributions will increase to meet claims as they become payable.

Of course, the other factor which might determine differentials between CNST contributions and premiums for employers' and public liability insurance is the amount of cover purchased (that is, the amount of risk transferred). This varies in relation to the structure of the risk-sharing agreement. A trust must choose (or be forced to accept) an excess on its policy which represents the initial sum it must pay from its own resources for each paid claim. Above this excess, the insurer/CNST agrees to pay a proportion of the trust's liability, which may be arranged in layers. The outcome of such structures is that trusts may face a large proportion of its low-value claims when settled, but a smaller proportion of the very high-value claims. Originally, the minimum excess available under the CNST was not discretionary, but depended upon the turnover of each trust. More recently, trusts have been taking the opportunity to reduce their excess levels:

> I think originally we couldn't go beneath [an excess of] £100,000 but now we have a £25,000 excess, and I think we could have had a £10,000 excess if we'd wanted it. The only reason we moved from £100,000 excess on CNST to £25,000 is that I did an exercise which showed, on our current database of claims, that by reducing the excess to that level the trust would ultimately benefit to the tune of £750,000.
> *(DF 10)*

Rather than ask technical questions about excesses, co-insurance and layers of cover, we presented the trusts with a set of hypothetical claim values and asked them to report how much of each claim they would have to meet themselves. The results in Table G4 indicate how cover tends to vary between liability lines for the average trust. For a £1,000,000 employer's or public liability claim, the insured trust typically has to find around 1 per cent of the settlement from its own resources, the remaining 99 per cent being met by the insurer. For EL or PL claims of £10,000, the proportion borne by the trust grows to 60–85 per cent. By comparison, clinical negligence risks are retained by the trust to a greater extent: some 10 per cent of £1,000,000 claims up to 100 per cent of £10,000 claims.

Table G4. Taking account of any excesses under the CNST and commercial insurance contracts, and allowing for any other pooling arrangements, please indicate how much the trust would have had to meet *itself* if an individual claim against the trust amounted to:

Individual liability claim (£)	*Clinical negligence*	*Employers' liability*	*Public liability*
10,000	10,000	8,568	5,889
50,000	34,428	11,210	7,908
100,000	47,500	11,233	7,868
1,000,000	101,866	11,233	7,868

A high proportion of claims are valued at £10,000 or less, indicating that, for clinical negligence at least, the aggregate level of uninsured liability payments exceeds those financed through the CNST and accounted for by the CNST subscriptions. For this reason, the accounting treatment of the uninsured liabilities is, and will remain, of considerable importance to trusts.

Of course, these *per risk* excesses mean that trusts are still exposed to the possibility of multiple claims (perhaps arising from a common clinical malpractice problem), with the excess payable on each and every one. We therefore asked trusts if they had any insurance protection against the accumulation risk arising from a series of individual claims in any one year. From the replies, eighteen had accumulation cover for employers' and public liability risks, but only eight thought that they had such cover for clinical negligence. This is a surprising finding in view of the spate of incidents where a faulty test or treatment or the actions of a negligent clinician have adversely affect many patients over a comparatively short period of time. This may be the reason why many trusts have been trying to reduce their *per risk* excess levels.

3.8 Number and value of claims

To put the accounting issues reviewed in this report into context, we asked each trust to provide figures for the stock of outstanding claims against them at the beginning and end of the 1998/99 financial year, as well as the flow of opened and closed claims during the year. This information was particularly important, given that there are no alternative sources available providing accurate current estimates of the volume of litigation against trusts. Tables H1 and H2 below show, as expected, a pattern of continuing growth in the stock of outstanding clinical negligence liabilities, by comparison with a smaller and relatively stable employers' and public liability claims experience. The proportion of claims that are closed with payment is much lower for clinical negligence claims (36 per cent of closed claims) than for other liabilities (65 per cent of closed claims), reflecting the evidential problems in proving fault in clinical cases. This finding confirms the importance of allowing for the closure of claims at zero cost when estimating provisions.

Table H1. Mean number of claims 1998/99[2]

	Outstanding at 31 March 1998	*Opened 1998/99 (to date)*	*Closed 1998/99 (to date)*		*Currently outstanding*
			With payment	*Without payment*	
Clinical negligence	75	31	12	22	81
Employers' liability	15	6	4	2	16
Public liability	3	2	1	1	3

2 A number of respondents only completed the right-hand column of tables H1 and H2, indicating the claims currently outstanding. For this reason, tables H1 and H2 do not necessarily cross-cast.

Table H2. Total number of claims 1998/99

	Outstanding at 31 March 1998	*Opened 1998/99 (to date)*	*Closed 1998/99 (to date)*		*Currently outstanding*
			With payment	*Without payment*	
Clinical negligence	3,820	1,570	558	997	4,211
Employers' liability	773	299	187	105	829
Public liability	135	81	59	28	143

Finally, the outcome of the processes we have reviewed in this report, together with the volume of litigation activity, is a set of internal and external financial accounts, some of which are placed in the public domain. Given the degree of discretion and consequent variation in practice that we have observed, it seems likely that the published financial data reflect these findings. In particular, we would expect the variations between trusts in reported clinical negligence provisions to reflect a combination of variations in litigation frequency and variations in the degree of accounting prudence adopted by the trust.

Table H3 summarises the accounting aggregates for clinical negligence for those trusts in our sample. There is considerable variation of I&E charges, provisions and contingent liabilities among the trusts in our sample. All the distributions are positively skewed (frequency distributions are shown in Appendix 10).

Table H3. Accounting aggregates for clinical negligence 1997/98 (66 trusts)

In £000	*I&E Charges*	*Provisions at 31 March 1998*		*Contingent liabilities*	
		Net	*Gross*	*Net*	*Gross*
Total	22,242	46,278	157,864	75,629	236,528
Mean	337	701	2,392	1,146	3,584
Std Devn	367	654	2,595	1,771	4,811

However, given the uncertainty surrounding the future costs of current claims, it is not immediately evident whether these variations are sufficient to make real, statistically significant differences to the reported aggregates in trust accounts. In particular, we do not know the extent to which the observed gross balance sheet provisions and contingent liabilities are partly a reflection of reporting discretion, and partly a reflection of the underlying frequency and severity of litigation.

To attempt an answer to this question using data from our survey of trusts, we undertook a statistical analysis of the relationship between reported accounting aggregates for clinical negligence and indicators of self-reported variations in practice from our survey, *controlling for the volume of litigation.* We did this by means of two ordinary least squares regressions, the results of which are reported in full in Appendix 11.

The results indicate that there is a significant systematic relationship between the financial liabilities of trusts attributed to clinical negligence, and the volume of such litigation. After controlling for this relationship, there is clear evidence that trusts' reported provisions and contingent liabilities are indeed sensitive to their discretionary treatment of claims. More specifically, the accounts were significantly influenced by decisions over borderline assessments of legal liability, but not by discretionary variations in the treatment of estimated quantum. Moreover, this impact is not small: those trusts which reported that they definitely *would* provide for claims assessed at 50 per cent liability declared a gross provision in 1997/98 of some £1.1 million more per trust than those which did not, after controlling for the volume of litigation. Turning to the disclosure of contingent liabilities, those trusts that allowed for the inclusion of part of those claims within provisions disclosed a lower level of contingencies of around £1.3 million per trust after controlling for the volume of litigation. These are sizeable figures, and serve to illustrate the importance of our findings.

4

Summary, Conclusions and Recommendations

We have established through this study that trusts face an increasing financial risk from the cumulative growth in legal liabilities arising from activities since their formation. Once these liabilities become known to trusts (that is, once claims are made), there remains a significant degree of uncertainty over whether and when a claim will settle, and at what cost to the trust. Managing this risk, particularly with respect to clinical negligence, is becoming an important task in which both accountants and claims managers have a role. Our findings have shed some light on the way these roles are being assigned within trusts, and the relationship between them.

The extent to which trusts transfer the claims management and claims financing roles to insurers or the NHSLA is partly a matter of managerial discretion, and partly a matter of the conditions imposed by the insurers. At present, we are concerned to note that there are adverse incentives present owing to the lack of true experience rating for CNST cover. As a consequence, CNST cover represents a 'good buy' for trusts that are aware that their risk and claims management procedures are inadequate. Once the full burden of clinical negligence has shifted from the health authorities and the ELS to the CNST, this problem will become more transparent as low-risk, well-managed trusts discover that their contribution rates rise disproportionately.

In relation to the reporting of legal liabilities which are retained rather than transferred to insurers, we have shown through both qualitative and quantitative analysis of data collected from trusts that there are considerable variations in accounting practice:

- The description of likelihood of liability used by trusts varied and was most commonly influenced by descriptions provided by trust solicitors. There seems to be a consensus that solicitors are not always willing to give firm predictions, and consequently a large number of claims are assessed at '50 per cent' or 'medium' likelihood of liability.
- Practice varies as to whether any claim which is assigned a probability of payment likelihood of exactly 50 per cent (or 'medium') should be provided in full, or partially or not at all.
- Where a claim is expected *never* to be paid (probability of liability of 0 per cent), almost 40 per cent of trusts said that they would still disclose the amount in their accounts as contingent liabilities.
- Some trusts were prepared to omit liabilities from the provision on the grounds that the quantum could not be assessed with reasonable accuracy.

- While the majority of trusts use the 'most likely' estimate of quantum, a significant minority opt for a more prudent 'worst-case' estimate.
- A minority of trusts adjust the aggregate of provisions and contingent liabilities, making reference to 'prudence' and 'realism' as a justification for doing so.

Moreover, we have established through statistical analysis of our survey data that these variations in practice are clearly related to significant differences in the accounting information. Consequently, we believe that this lack of consistency is hindering performance comparisons between trusts, and effective risk management procedures within each trust. Lack of consistency in accounting for claims at trust level creates uncertainty in the interpretation of the consolidated accounts of the NHS and the use of such accounting information to inform policy debate.

We believe that the adoption of greater consistency in the accounting for risk in the NHS would therefore be desirable. As we have seen, there are indeed attempts already in place to provide trusts with guidelines for appropriate practice. However, it seems that the interpretation of these guidelines in terms of the adoption of an 'expected-value' approach to provisions, and a 'worst-case' scenario for contingent liabilities, is not always consistent. A closer liaison between trust solicitors, claims managers and accountants is needed to ensure that the claims are considered on a case-by-case basis and that liability and quantum estimates are updated regularly.

More specifically, we recommend that good claims management practice involves the following:

- Solicitors acting for trusts should be encouraged to provide and regularly update, for each claim, an estimate of the trust's liability within well-defined numerical ranges (i.e. not simply 0–50 per cent and 50–100 per cent), bearing in mind the fact that two-thirds of all claims are typically closed without payment.[1] Solicitors should also provide and regularly update, for each claim, a best estimate of quantum, and a worst-case estimate, on the assumption that the trust is liable.
- Trusts should use this information to calculate aggregate gross provisions on an expected-value basis: that is, they should multiply each claim's estimated probability of liability by the best estimate of quantum, and then sum these products over all claims.
- Trusts should calculate aggregate gross contingencies on the basis of a worst-case scenario for all claims with a non-remote chance of liability (in effect, all those which have a non-zero assessment of liability by solicitors). The contingent liability note should be based upon these worst-case estimates of quantum after deducting an amount for any provision made.

1 The current proposal to estimate FRS 12 provisions on the basis of 25 per cent for those assessed between 0 per cent and 50 per cent would result in a provision being made for all such claims. A separate category of 'very low liability' or an equivalent is essential in order to minimise this problem.

- As their claims experience builds, trusts should work towards the creation of a claims database held locally and also pooled nationally through the NHSLA. These databases would then inform trusts' decisions over provisions and contingencies in future years, as well as enabling them to monitor the outcome of predictions over liability and quantum.

Obviously, current guidance to accountants has to steer a course between excessive reliance on subjective estimates of likelihood, which are difficult to monitor in the auditing process, and inadequate clarity over when and how much to provide when the validity of claims is in doubt. In the long run, once a reasonably stable claims experience has emerged for trusts, the answer may well lie in taking a view about the likely distribution of settlements overall, as opposed to a simple aggregate of individual claims.

Finally, it is clear to us that the management accountant's role in the processes discussed above is central. Claims information is one of the most important indicators of service quality and patient satisfaction available to trust managers. The collection and organisation of these data facilitate internal decisions over risk transfer, risk retention and risk avoidance measures. They also inform negotiations between providers and health care commissioners in relation to service agreements and costs. This project has shed some light on the diversity of practice between trusts. We hope our findings can be interpreted as both a warning and an opportunity for management accountants in the health sector.

Appendix 1 Letter Requesting Interviews

1 June 1998

Dear (Director of Finance)

Accounting for Risk in the NHS (a CIMA-funded research project)

We have recently been awarded a grant from the Chartered Institute of Management Accountants to research the process of accounting for the major legal liabilities which confront NHS trusts. The research proposal was developed in conjunction with (Name), Director of Corporate Affairs, at the (General Acute Unit NHS Trust).

(General Acute Unit NHS Trust) is the site of our preliminary, and most detailed, inquiries. We are currently collecting a range of qualitative and quantitative data which will form the basis of a case study. In the second phase of the project we intend to extend the study to other trusts, where we propose to discuss issues concerning clinical negligence and public and employers' liabilities, and their associated insurance coverage, with the relevant managers.

We are writing both to inform you of this research, as well as to ask for your co-operation. At this stage we are particularly interested in locating a sample of trusts which would be interested in taking part in the second phase. We would like to include trusts from different regions and are as interested in those with below-average contingencies/provisions as those with higher figures. We plan to conduct semi-structured, tape-recorded interviews with the key individuals involved in the claims/accountancy process. This would probably mean three interviews in each trust – with the finance director, the management/financial accountant and the claims manager. However, none of these should last longer than an hour. We would emphasise that all material will be treated as confidential and that individual trusts will not be identifiable in any resulting publications. All participating trusts will be given feedback in relation to the project's findings.

If you are interested in taking part in this research or would like any further information, please contact our Research Associate, Pamela Watson.

Tel 0115 951 5094
Fax 0115 951 5098
e-mail pamela.watson@nottingham.ac.uk

Yours sincerely

Paul Fenn, Norwich Union Professor of Insurance Studies
Steve Diacon, Senior Lecturer in Insurance
Ron Hodges, Lecturer in Accountancy

Appendix 2 Director of Finance Interview Guide

1. Explanation of project.

2. Ask about relative importance of risks facing the trust – particularly those relating to clinical negligence, employer liability and public liability.

3. Who is – or has been – involved in decisions about insurance cover (ask about excess levels)
   - any significant changes recently (why?)
   - more specifically, how were/are decisions made about joining and remaining with CNST?

4. How are risks identified, and costs recognised and valued for internal reporting purposes?
   - who are main people involved?

5. What information is made available to the trust board and to various risk committees (how/when)?
   - exact role of finance department?
   - how are changing circumstances reflected in reports?
   - have these procedures changed over the recent past?

6. (Go on to external reporting.)
   Financial targets – relative importance of each
   How are figures for costs, provisions and contingencies determined?
   (– finance department, solicitors, loss adjusters etc.)
   - evidence used to provide the valuations?
   - auditors check any of this?
   - any recent changes?

7. Questioning of these figures by trust board?

8. Any other issues, most important issue.

Appendix 3 Management Accountant Interview Guide

Describe briefly the nature of the research project.
Start with CN, but relate to EL and PL when appropriate.

1. How do you (the accountant) first get to hear of potential or actual claims? What happens as a result?

2 What information, and in what form, do you anticipate passing on to:
- others in the finance department?
- the trust board?
- various committees (which ones and why)?

How regularly is this done either *(a)* formally though a written report; or *(b)* informally? How do these reports show CN, EL and PL costs?

3. How are decisions made regarding whether the cost of a claim is *(a)* included in reports as a cost/liability, *(b)* included as a contingent (potential) liability; or *(c)* ignored as being too remote to include in the report?

4. To what extent does the trust rely upon its solicitors to provide estimates of quantum and probability of liability? [Try to discover whether the trust uses schedules from solicitors to reflect figures in the accounting reports.] To what extent are figures adjusted in moving from the solicitors' schedules to the accounting reports?

5. What information and evidence do your auditors require to verify the figures for costs/provisions and contingent liability notes?

6. How does the trust go about recovering its costs from purchasers? Is it based upon the reported costs and provisions or is it based upon cash paid out to meet these claims or some combination? [The issue here is whether it is possible to recover these costs as they are reported for income and expenditure purposes, or whether recovery in prices is only realistic at the time, or after, cash payment is made to the claimant.]

7. Are the estimated costs of CN, EL and PL allocated to budgets of individual directorates? What is the basis of allocation or apportionment? Is it the estimated costs or cash payments that drive this allocation?

8. [Raise here some issues concerning insurance cover but be aware that the accountant may not play a direct role here.] Is your trust a member of CNST? How was the decision (not) to join made? What excess levels for insurance have been chosen? Why were these levels chosen?

9. Are there other issues in managing and reporting clinical negligence costs that you think we might wish to include in our further work in this project?

Appendix 4 Claims Manager Interview Guide

1. Explanation of project.

2. Responsibilities of claims manager. How does post fit into the management structure in this trust?
Development of current system. Relationship to complaints.

3. Are the things we are particularly interested in treated together – part of overall concept of risk – or as separate entities? Who else involved? Differences in how handled?

4. Decisions about CNST (details of payments, excess levels), insurance companies, lawyers.
(Use of brokers, loss adjusters.) Who decides and how and why?

5. (Approximate) numbers of cases currently being considered?
Use of database (clinical negligence/PL/EL)?
(other recording systems?)

6. Liaison/communications with legal advisers (insurers).
Who makes initial assessments re. likely outcome – liability and costs?
In what circumstances would these be modified?

7. Liaison/communication with finance dept.
How and at what point is claims information passed on to finance?
Explore procedures for notifying finance of changes (routine or extraordinary).

8. Liaison with CNST.

9. Settlement: Who is involved in determining *(a)* timing of offer; *(b)* amount of offer?
Who determines factors such as payments into court? Closure without payment.
Are there types/values of claim your department would be authorised to settle (and who authorises)?

10. Costs (In what ways do you try to limit your own costs? Are these separated from total costs?).

11. Any other important issues.

Appendix 5 Letter Issued with Pilot Questionnaire

Tel. 0115 951 5269
e-mail pamela.watson@nottingham.ac.uk

28 January 1999

Dear (Director of Finance)

Accounting for Risk in the NHS

We visited your trust last September and interviewed you, and two of your colleagues, as part of our research into the management and accounting processes for clinical negligence, and employers' and public liability claims. We very much appreciated your help then, and now wonder if we could ask for a little more.

Having analysed all the interview material we are almost ready to progress to the final part of the study. This takes the form of a questionnaire, which we intend to send to all NHS hospital trusts in England. However, before we do this we hope that you might be prepared to comment on a preliminary version. There is no need to complete the questions but perhaps you, or another member of the finance department, could read through it and advise us if what we are asking for is both reasonable and clearly expressed. I am also enclosing a draft copy of the accompanying letter. We would be quite satisfied if you were to write on the document itself – we don't need a formal letter – and there is a freepost envelope provided, although if you would rather telephone or e-mail that would be fine.

We would certainly value your input into this important part of our research.

Yours sincerely

Paul Fenn	Norwich Union Professor of Insurance Studies
Steve Diacon	Professor of Insurance Management
Ron Hodges	Lecturer in Accounting and Finance
Pamela Watson	Research Associate

Appendix 6 Questionnaire

University of Nottingham Accounting for Risk in the NHS

Trust Name...

Please answer all the questions. All replies will be treated with the strictest confidence.

Section A	*Please provide information about your Trust's management and administrative structures.*

A1. Is the Director of Finance (or another representative of the Accounting/Finance Department) a member of the following Trust committees? Please provide the exact title of the committee in the third column (if you have no such committee please write 'None')

Committee	Finance Member: Yes or No?	Exact Committee Title
Clinical Risk Management		
Clinical Audit		
Non-Clinical Risk		
Health & Safety		

A2. Which individual/department is *principally* responsible for the handling of clinical negligence, employers' liability and public liability claims for the Trust? Please indicate if principal responsibility for the work lies with an outside agency.

	Title of relevant individual or department	Details of any outside agency
Clinical Negligence		
Employers' Liability		
Public Liability		

A3. Is your Trust responsible for handling the clinical negligence, employers' liability or public liability claims of other Trusts or Health Authorities?

	Other Trusts: Yes or No?	HA: Yes or No?
Clinical Negligence		
Employers' Liability		
Public Liability		

Section B ***Please provide information about the LIKELIHOOD OF LIABILITY and QUANTUM in the estimation of Clinical Negligence, Employers' Liability or Public Liability claims.***

B1. How does the Finance Department (or Claims Management Department if appropriate) record information on the *likelihood of liability* for a particular claim?

Please tick one box in each column.	**Clinical Negligence**	**Employers' Liability**	**Public Liability**
As a percentage probability of liability (e.g. 0-5%, 5-50%, 50%-95%)			
As a category representing probability of liability (e.g. low, medium, high)			
Both			
Neither – different system used			

B2. What action is taken in the light of information on the likelihood of liability when deciding whether to make a gross *provision* (i.e. before recovery from CNST/ELS or other insurers) for an individual claim in the Trust's financial accounts?

Please tick one box for each row in the table.		**Action**		
Percentage likelihood of Trust liability	If you use a different system for likelihood please give categories here and show how they correspond to the first column	**Definitely provide**	**Definitely do *not* provide**	***May provide**
0%				
Over 0% but under 50%				
50%				
Over 50% but under 95%				
95% and over.				

* If you ticked the 'May provide' box for any of the categories in the previous question please explain the factors that determine whether or not to provide for that claim

....

....

B3. What action is taken in the light of information on the likelihood of liability when deciding whether to include part or all of an individual claim as a gross *contingent liability* (i.e. before recovery from CNST/ELS or other insurers) in the Trust's financial accounts?

Please tick one box for each row in the table.		Action		
Percentage likelihood of Trust liability	If you use a different system for likelihood please give categories here and show how they correspond to the first column	**Definitely include as a contingent liability**	**Definitely do *not* include as a contingent liability**	***May include as contingent liability**
0%				
Over 0% but under 50%				
50%				
Over 50% but under 95%				
95% and over.				

* If you ticked the '*May include*' box for any of the categories in the previous question please explain the factors that determine whether or not to include part or all of the claim as a contingent liability

....

....

B4. How does the Finance Department (or Claims Management Department) record information on the estimated quantum (i.e. gross claims payable) and legal or associated costs for a particular claim?

Please tick all boxes that apply.	**Quantum**	**Trust's Legal Costs**	**Claimant's Legal Costs**
Best case estimate (minimum gross loss to Trust)			
Worst case estimate (maximum gross loss to Trust)			
Most likely estimate			
No estimate recorded			
None of the above (please explain)			
....			
....			

B5. Which of these estimates of quantum is used when estimating the amount to be included as a gross *provision* (i.e. before recovery from CNST/ELS or other insurers) for a particular claim in the Trust's financial accounts?

Please tick one box.	**Unweighted**	**Weighted by likelihood of liability**
Best case estimate		
Worst case estimate		
Most likely estimate		
None of the above (please explain)		
....		
....		

B6. Which of these estimates of quantum is used when estimating the amount to be included as a gross *contingent liability* (i.e. before recovery from CNST/ELS or other insurers) for a particular claim in the Note to the Trust's financial accounts?

Please tick one box.	**With a deduction for the provision**	**Without a deduction for the provision**
Best case estimate		
Worst case estimate		
Most likely estimate		
None of the above (please explain)		

....

....

Section C ***Please provide information about how the resulting TOTAL PROVISIONS AND CONTINGENCY NOTE for Clinical Negligence, Employers' Liability and Public Liability are determined for the purposes of annual financial accounting.***

C1. What assumptions are made about any recoveries* under relevant insurance contracts in computing the provisions and contingent liabilities in the Trust's financial accounts?
Please tick one box in each column.

* Recovery means recovery from insurers in line with the terms and conditions of the contract, taking into account any excesses or deductibles

Provisions	**Clinical Negligence**	**Employers' Liability**	**Public Liability**
Complete recovery assumed			
No recovery assumed			
Other (please explain)			

....

....

Contingencies	**Clinical Negligence**	**Employers' Liability**	**Public Liability**
Complete recovery assumed			
No recovery assumed			
Other (please explain)			

....

....

The remaining questions in this section assume that insurance recoveries are included, and the questions talk about *net* provisions and contingent liabilities (i.e. net of recoveries).

C2. *For the financial year ending 31/3/98*, was the Trust's net aggregate provision equal to the sum of the net provisions on individual cases, or was this sum adjusted before inclusion in the financial accounts? Please tick one box.

Sum included without further adjustment	
Sum included after a further adjustment – upwards	
Sum included after a further adjustment – downwards	

C3. If an adjustment was made to obtain the net provision, what factors influence this adjustment? Tick any box that applied.

Requirement to achieve breakeven on Income and Expenditure	
Requirement to meet EFL target	
Requirement of 6% return on net assets	
Need to be prudent in estimating provisions	
Need to be realistic in estimating provisions	
Pressure from purchasers/commissioners	
Pressure from members of Trust Board	
Pressure from Trust's Audit Committee	
Pressure from Trust's external auditor	
Other (please explain)	

C4. *For the financial year ending 31/3/98* was the net contingent liability equal to the sum of the individual cases or was this sum adjusted before inclusion in the financial accounts? Please tick one box.

Sum included without further adjustment	
Sum included after a further adjustment – upwards	
Sum included after a further adjustment – downwards	

C5. If such an adjustment was made to obtain the net contingent liability, what factors influence this adjustment? Tick any box that applied.

Need to be prudent in estimating contingent liabilities	
Need to be realistic in estimating contingent liabilities	
Pressure from purchasers/commissioners	
Pressure from members of Trust Board	
Pressure from Trust's Audit Committee	
Pressure from Trust's external auditors	
Other (please explain)	

C6. Is any explicit figure included in the aggregate provisions or contingent liabilities for potential claims that have not yet been notified to the Trust? YES / NO

If YES, please say where this figure is included in the Accounts and describe briefly how it is calculated.

....

Section D	***Please provide information about the extent to which clinical negligence, employers' and public liability costs are included in BUDGETS (planned expenditure).***

D1. How are the *insurance premiums* for clinical negligence, employers' and public liability incorporated in your Trust's budgeting system?

Please tick one box for each column.	**Clinical Negligence**	**Employers' Liability**	**Public Liability**
Premiums not included in budgets at any level			
Premiums included in budgets as central overheads and not allocated to particular clinical directorates			
Premiums included in the budgets of specific clinical directorates, but not allocated to specific service activities			
Premiums included in the budgets as a direct cost of related service activity			
Other methods of budgeting (please explain)			

D2. How is an allowance for *'uninsured' losses* arising from clinical negligence, employers' and public liability incorporated in your Trust's budgeting system?

Please tick one box for each column.	**Clinical Negligence**	**Employers' Liability**	**Public Liability**
Costs not included in budgets at any level			
Costs included in budgets as central overheads and not allocated to particular clinical directorates			
Costs included in the budgets of specific clinical directorates, but not allocated to specific service activities			
Costs included in the budgets as a direct cost of related service activity			
Other methods (please explain)			

Section E	*Please provide information about the extent to which ACTUAL clinical negligence, employers' and public liability costs are allocated in management accounts.*

E1. How are the *insurance premiums* for clinical negligence, employers' and public liability allocated in your Trust's management accounting system?

Please tick one box for each column.	**Clinical Negligence**	**Employers' Liability**	**Public Liability**
Premiums treated as central overheads and not allocated to particular clinical directorates			
Premiums treated as overheads of specific clinical directorate to which claim relates, but not allocated to specific service activities			
Premiums treated as a direct cost of service activity to which claim relates			
Other methods (please explain)			

E2. How are the *'uninsured' losses* for clinical negligence, employers' and public liability allocated in your Trust's management accounting system?

Please tick one box for each column.	**Clinical Negligence**	**Employers' Liability**	**Public Liability**
Costs treated as central overheads and not allocated to particular clinical directorates			
Costs treated as overheads to the specific clinical directorate to which claim relates, but not allocated to specific service activities			
Costs treated as a direct cost of the service activity to which claim relates			
Other methods (please explain)			

Section F ***Please provide information about the recovery of clinical negligence, employers' and public liability costs through the PRICES CHARGED TO YOUR PURCHASERS or COMMISSIONERS.***

F1. How is the Trust's contribution to the CNST, and the insurance premiums paid to commercial insurers, *recovered* from purchasers?

Please tick one box for each column.	**CNST**	**Employers' Liability**	**Public Liability**
Purchasers do not accept this cost			
Purchasers have agreed to make a specific cash settlement to cover this cost either in year of accrual or at a later date			
Cost is identified separately and included in overall price structure			
Cost is included in the overall price structure although not identified separately			
Other (please explain)			

F2. How does the Trust recover the '*uninsured*' costs of clinical negligence, employers' liability and public liability claims from purchasers?

Please tick one box for each column.	**Clinical Negligence**	**Employers' Liability**	**Public Liability**
Purchasers have not accepted this cost			
Purchasers make a cash settlement to cover the cost *in the year of accrual*			
Purchasers have agreed to make a cash settlement to cover the cost *at a later date* (e.g. at the time of payment)			
The *accrued* cost is identified separately and included in the overall price structure			
The *expected settlement cost* for the coming period is identified separately and included in the overall price structure			
The *accrued* cost is included in the overall price structure, although not identified separately			
The *expected settlement cost* for the coming period is included in the overall price structure although not identified separately			
Other (please explain)			

Section G	*Please provide some information about your INSURANCE ARRANGEMENTS.*

G1. Is the Trust a member of the Clinical Negligence Scheme for Trusts (CNST)? YES / NO

If yes, please provide:	1997/8	1998/9
Annual contribution £		
CNST Risk Management Standard		

G2. Is the Trust insured against Employers' liability claims? YES / NO

If yes, please provide:	1997/8	1998/9
Annual premium £		

G3. Is the Trust insured against Public liability claims? YES / NO

If yes, please provide:	1997/8	1998/9
Annual premium £		

G4. Taking account of any excesses under the CNST and commercial insurance contracts, and allowing for any other pooling arrangements, please indicate how much the Trust would have had to meet *itself* if an individual claim against the Trust amounted to:

Individual liability claim £	**Clinical Negligence**	**Employers' Liability**	**Public Liability**
10 000			
50 000			
100 000			
1 000 000			

G5. Does the Trust have any insurance protection to cover the accumulation risk arising from a series of individual claims in any one year?

Please tick if 'yes'	**Clinical Negligence**	**Employers' Liability**	**Public Liability**
Accumulation cover?			

Section II ***Please provide information about the NUMBER of liability claims against your Trust***

	Outstanding at March 31 1998	Opened 1998/99 (to date)	Closed 1998/9 (to date)		Currently outstanding
			With payment	Without payment	
Clinical Negligence					
Employers' Liability					
Public Liability					

Today's Date: ....

Thank you very much for completing this questionnaire

Please return the completed questionnaire, in the enclosed pre-paid addressed envelope, to:

Dr P Watson
University of Nottingham Business School
University Park
Nottingham
NG7 2RD

Tel: 0115 951 5269
Fax: 0115 951 5262
e-mail pam.watson@nottingham.ac.uk

Appendix 7 Letter Issued with Questionnaire

19 March 1999

Dear (Director of Finance)

Accounting for Risk in the NHS

You will be aware of attempts to regulate the accounting treatment of provisions and contingencies within the NHS and, on a broader level, by the Accounting Standards Board. We are currently engaged in a CIMA-sponsored research project which has, as its focus, those issues confronting trusts in dealing with the management of, and accounting for, clinical negligence and employer and public liability claims. These claims present particular challenges in view of their uncertain value and timing. We anticipate that our study will provide further insight into the issues facing managers and accountants in NHS trusts and will help to inform debate of developments in this area.

We are asking for your help in completing the enclosed questionnaire, which is being sent to all NHS hospital trusts in England. Earlier stages of our project have indicated that there is considerable diversity across trusts in the way these claims are valued and accounted for. We are attempting now to gain an understanding of procedures adopted by a wider selection of trusts.

The questionnaire is aimed principally at the finance department, although the final section may require additional input from the claims department. Most questions may be answered by ticking appropriate boxes rather than needing full narrative. The name of your trust has been included in order to minimise requests for background information. We wish to emphasise that all information will be treated as confidential and no individual respondent or organisation will be identified in any published work.

We will supply all respondents with a summary of the results of our analysis, which we believe will provide helpful benchmarking information for management purposes. If you require any further information about the project, or if queries arise from the questionnaire, please do not hesitate to contact Pamela Watson by post, telephone or e-mail.

We have enclosed a freepost envelope for your completed questionnaire.

Thank you for your help.

Yours sincerely

Paul Fenn	Norwich Union Professor of Insurance Studies
Steve Diacon	Professor of Insurance Management
Ron Hodges	Senior Lecturer in Accounting and Finance
Pamela Watson	Research Associate

Appendix 8 Reminder Letter with Questionnaire

Tel. 0115 951 5269
e-mail pamela.watson@nottingham.ac.uk

22 April 1999

Dear (Finance Director)

First reminder: Questionnaire on Accounting for Risk in the NHS

About a month ago we sent you a questionnaire as part of a CIMA-sponsored research project which has, as its focus, those issues confronting trusts in dealing with the management of, and accounting for, clinical negligence and employer and public liability claims.

As we are very anxious to obtain as comprehensive a response as possible to our survey we are sending you a duplicate copy of the questionnaire. We would be very grateful if you could find the time to complete this. However, if you have already posted the original we apologise for this reminder.

The questionnaire is aimed principally at the finance department, although the final section may require additional input from the claims department. Most questions may be answered by ticking appropriate boxes rather than needing full narrative. The name of your trust has been included in order to minimise requests for background information. We wish to emphasise that all information will be treated as confidential and no individual respondent or organisation will be identified in any published work.

We will supply all respondents with a summary of the results of our analysis, which we believe will provide helpful benchmarking information for management purposes. If you require any further information about the project, or if queries arise from the questionnaire, please do not hesitate to contact Pamela Watson by post, telephone or e-mail.

We have enclosed a freepost envelope for your completed questionnaire.

Thank you for your help.

Yours sincerely

Paul Fenn	Norwich Union Professor of Insurance Studies
Steve Diacon	Professor of Insurance Management
Ron Hodges	Senior Lecturer in Accounting and Finance
Pamela Watson	Research Associate

Appendix 9
Comparison of Sample and Population Characteristics

Trusts by type

Type		*Non-respondents*	*Sample*	*Population*
Multiple Activity	Count	41	21	62
	% within sample	23.8%	31.8%	26.1%
General Acute	Count	115	38	153
	% within sample	66.9%	57.6%	64.3%
Specialist	Count	16	7	23
	% within sample	9.3%	10.6%	9.7%
Total	Count	172	66	238
	% within sample	100.0%	100.0%	100.0%

Trusts by region

Region		*Non-respondents*	*Sample*	*Population*
Anglia & Oxford	Count	16	8	24
	% within sample	9.3%	12.1%	10.1%
North Thames	Count	33	5	38
	% within sample	19.2%	7.6%	16.0%
North West	Count	23	15	38
	% within sample	13.4%	22.7%	16.0%
Northern & Yorks	Count	21	10	31
	% within sample	12.2%	15.2%	13.0%
South Thames	Count	25	7	32
	% within sample	14.5%	10.6%	13.4%
South & West	Count	20	5	25
	% within sample	11.6%	7.6%	10.5%
Trent	Count	11	12	23
	% within sample	6.4%	18.2%	9.7%
West Midlands	Count	23	4	27
	% within sample	13.4%	6.1%	11.3%
Total	Count	172	66	238
	% within sample	100.0%	100.0%	100.0%

Trusts by wave

Wave		*Non-respondents*	*Sample*	*Population*
1	Count	29	11	40
	% within sample	16.9%	16.7%	16.8%
2	Count	35	16	51
	% within sample	20.3%	24.2%	21.4%
3	Count	53	22	75
	% within sample	30.8%	33.3%	31.5%
4	Count	50	15	65
	% within sample	29.1%	22.7%	27.3%
5	Count	5	2	7
	% within sample	2.9%	3.0%	2.9%
Total	Count	172	66	238
	% within sample	100.0%	100.0%	100.0%

Trusts by financial aggregates

		Assets 1998	*Gross provisions 1998*	*Gross contingencies 1998*
Population	Mean	62421	2865	2162
	N	172	172	172
	Std deviation	38802	2666	5633
Sample	Mean	60866	2392	3584
	N	66	66	66
	Std deviation	35574	2595	4811
Total	Mean	61941	2734	2557
	N	238	238	238
	Std deviation	37935	2647	5418

Note: There were 64 questionnaire responses representing 66 trusts prior to mergers in 1999/2000. A total of 221 questionnaires were issued representing 238 trusts prior to mergers in 1999/2000.

Appendix 10 Frequency Distributions of Accounting Data

Clinical negligence charges in 1997/98 I&E of questionnaire respondents

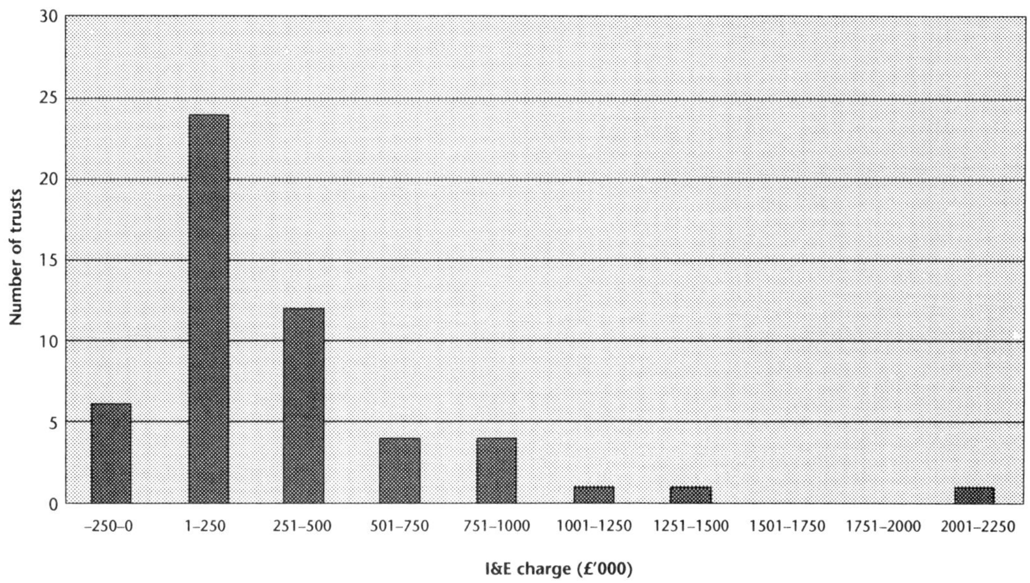

Gross clinical negligence provisions at 31 March 1998 of questionnaire respondents

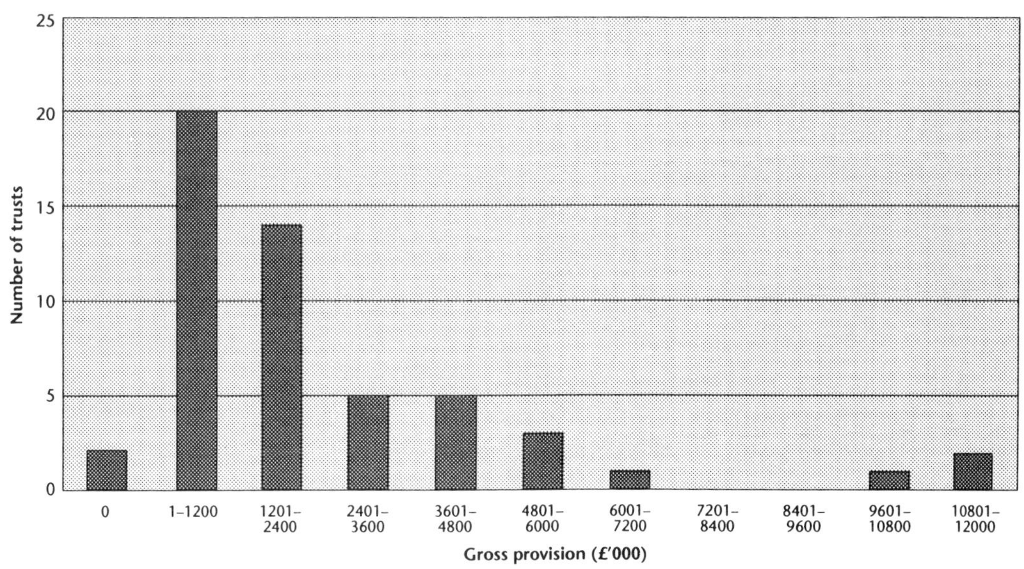

Clinical negligence charges in 1997/98 I&E of questionnaire respondents

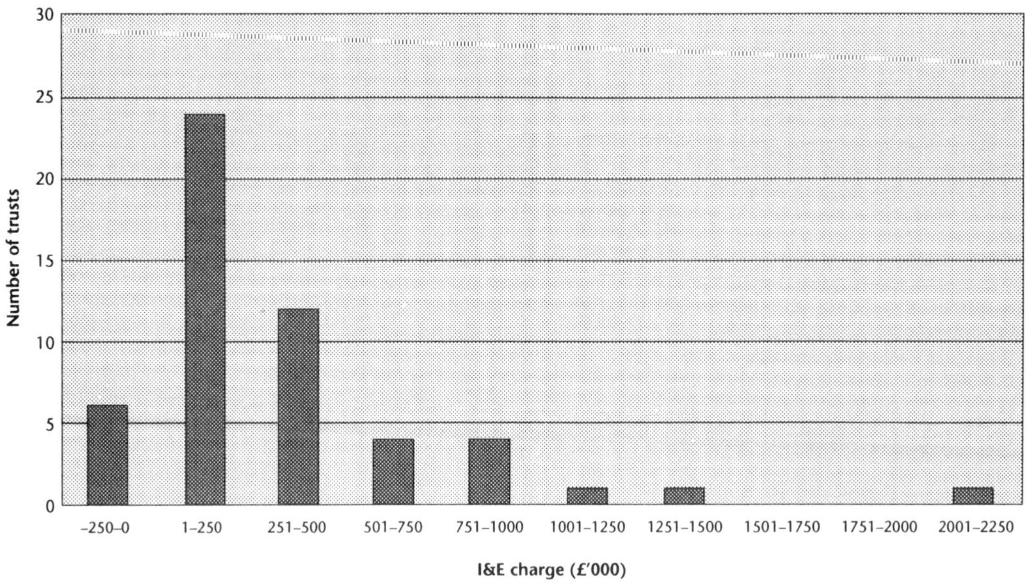

Gross contingent liabilities at 31 March 1998 of questionnaire respondents

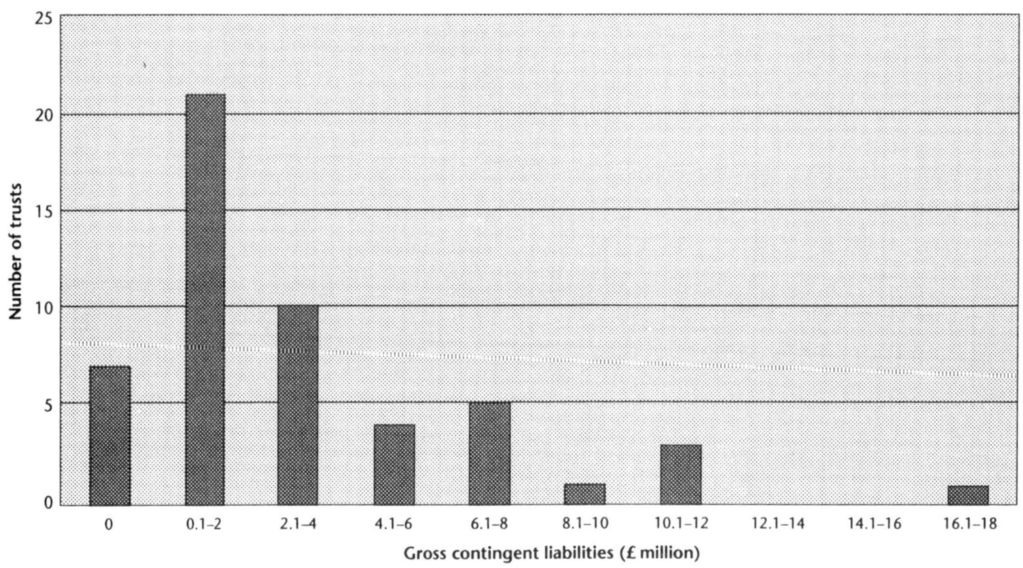

Net contingent liabilities at 31 March 1998 of questionnaire respondents

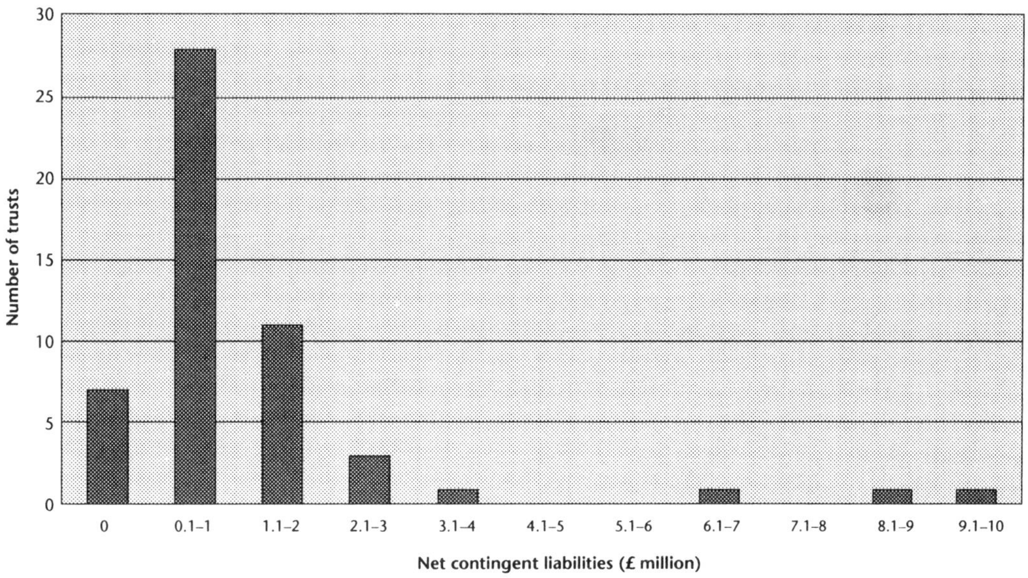

Appendix 11 Regression Results

Gross provisions 1997/98

GRPROV98 = Gross provisions 1997/8

H1A = Outstanding claims 1997/8

B2G = 1 if trust provides for 50% liabilities, 0 otherwise

B5COMP = 1 if trust does not discount quantum to reflect liability, 0 otherwise

B5WORS = 1 if trust uses worst-case estimates of quantum, 0 otherwise

Coefficients[a]

		Unstandardised coefficients		*Standardised coefficients*		
Model		*B*	*Std error*	*Beta*	*t*	*Sig.*
1	(Constant)	208.184	768.425		0.271	0.788
	H1A	20.194	5.506	0.470	3.667	0.001
	B2G	1122.773	614.264	0.237	1.828	0.074
	B5COMP	44.334	650.876	0.009	0.068	0.946
	B5WORS	–904.041	791.263	–0.149	–1.143	0.259

a. Dependent variable: GRPROV98

Model summary

Model	*R*	*R square*	*Adjusted R square*	*Std error of the estimate*
1	0.532[a]	0.283	0.218	2097.581

a. Predictors: (constant), B5WORS, H1A, B5COMP, B2G

ANOVA[b]

Model		*Sum of squares*	*df*	*Mean square*	*F*	*Sig.*
1	Regression	7.6E+07	4	1.9E+07	4.345	0.005[a]
	Residual	1.9E+08	44	4.4E+07		
	Total	2.7E+08	48			

a. Predictors: (constant), B5WORS, H1A, B5COMP, B2G

b. Dependent variable: GRPROV98

Gross contingent liabilities 1997/8

CONTGRSS = Gross contingent liabilities 1997/8

H1A = Outstanding claims 1997/8

B3A = 1 if trust discloses 0% liabilities, 0 otherwise

B6COMP = 1 if trust does not deduct for provisions, 0 otherwise

B6WORS = 1 if trust uses worst-case estimates of quantum, 0 otherwise

Coefficients[a]

		Unstandardised coefficients		*Standardised coefficients*		
Model		*B*	*Std error*	*Beta*	*t*	*Sig.*
1	(Constant)	–525.116	997.250		–0.527	0.601
	H1A	25.335	9.522	0.366	2.661	0.011
	B3A	1302.965	1034.399	0.170	1.260	0.214
	B6COMP	1267.232	766.564	0.225	1.653	0.105
	B6WORS	180.640	1123.510	0.021	0.161	0.873

a. Dependent variable: CONTGRSS

Model summary

Model	*R*	*R square*	*Adjusted R square*	*Std error of the estimate*
1	0.514[a]	0.265	0.199	3386.94

a. Predictors: (constant), B6WORS, B6COMP, B3A, H1A

ANOVA[b]

Model		*Sum of squares*	*df*	*Mean square*	*F*	*Sig.*
1	Regression	1.8E+08	4	4.6E+07	4.049	0.007[a]
	Residual	5.2E+08	45	1.1E+07		
	Total	7.0E+08	49			

a. Predictors: (constant), B6WORS,B6COMP, B3A, H1A

b. Dependent variable: CONTGRSS

Note: Some respondents did not provide the necessary information to allow inclusion in this analysis.

References

ASB (1994), *Financial Reporting Standard 5: Reporting the Substance of Transactions,* Accounting Standards Board, London.

ASB (1998), *Financial Reporting Standard 12: Provisions and Contingencies,* Accounting Standards Board, London.

ASC (1980), *Statement of Standard Accounting Practice 18: Accounting for Contingencies,* Accounting Standards Committee, London.

Baldwin, R (ed.) (1997), *Law and Uncertainty: Risks and Legal Processes,* Kluwer Law International, London.

Dowding, T (1996), 'Small claims handling in NHS Trusts', *Health Care Risk Report,* July/August, 4–5.

Farber, H S and White, M J (1991), 'Medical malpractice: an empirical examination of the litigation process', *RAND Journal of Economics,* 22, 2, 199–217.

Farber, H S and White, M J (1994), 'A comparison of formal and informal dispute resolution in medical malpractice', *Journal of Legal Studies,* 23, 2, 777–806.

Fenn, P and Dingwall, R (1991), 'The role of information in medical litigation' in Fenn, P and Dingwall, R (eds) *Quality and Regulation in Health Care: International Perspectives,* Routledge.

Fenn, P and Rickman, N (1999), 'Delay and settlement in litigation', *Economic Journal,* 109, 457, 476–91.

HCIS (1995–99), *The Fitzhugh Directory of NHS Trusts: Financial Information,* 3rd, 4th, 5th, 6th and 7th editions, Health Care Information Services, London.

Hodges, R (1999), 'Problems with provisions', *The Fitzhugh Directory of NHS Trusts 1999,* A17–A21, HCIS, London.

Hughes, J W and Savoca, E (1997), 'Measuring the effect of legal reforms on the longevity of medical malpractice claims', *International Review of Law and Economics,* 17, 2, 261–73.

LCD (1999), *The Impact of Plaintiff Finance on Personal Injury Litigation,* Research Report, Lord Chancellor's Department.

NAO (1997), Report of the Comptroller and Auditor General on the NHS (England) Summarised Accounts 1995–96, HC 127, 18 July 1997, HMSO, London.

NAO (1998), Report of the Comptroller and Auditor General on the NHS (England) Summarised Accounts 1996–97, HC 923, 21 July 1998, HMSO, London.

NAO (1999), 'NHS (England) Summarised Accounts 1997–98', *National Audit Office Press Notice,* 7 May 1999.

NHSE (1994), *NHS Trust Manual of Accounts 1994/95,* FDL(94)74, NHS Executive, Leeds.

NHSE (1996a), *NHS Trust Manual of Accounts 1996/97,* FDL(96)07, NHS Executive, Leeds.

NHSE (1996b), *NHS Trusts' Pricing for Provisions and Similar Costs,* FDL(96)38, NHS Executive, Leeds

NHSE (1997), *NHS Trust Manual of Accounts 1997/98,* FDL(97)13, NHS Executive, Leeds.

NHSE (1998a), *NHS Trusts' Recovery of Provisions and Similar Costs,* HSC 1998/105, NHS Executive, Leeds.

NHSE (1998b), *NHS Trust Manual of Accounts 1998/99,* HSC 1998/184, NHS Executive, Leeds.

NHSE (1998c), *Insurance in the NHS,* HSC 1998/174, NHS Executive, Leeds.

NHSE (1998d), *Handling Clinical Negligence Claims,* HSC 1998/183, NHS Executive, Leeds.

NHSE (1999a), *NHS Trust Accounts End of Year Letter,* 30 March 1999, NHS Executive, Leeds.

NHSE (1999b), *Guidance to Health Authorities and NHS Trusts on Break-even Duty, Provisions and Accumulated Deficits,* HSC 1999/146, NHS Executive, Leeds.

NHSE (1999c), *NHS Trusts and Health Authorities: FRS 12, Provisions, Contingent Liabilities and Contingent Assets,* HSC 1999/174, NHS Executive, Leeds.

NHSE (1999d), *Insurance in the NHS: Employers'/Public Liability and Miscellaneous Risk Pooling,* HSC 1999/021, NHS Executive, Leeds.

Sloan, F A and Hoerger, T J (1991), 'Uncertainty, information, and the resolution of medical malpractice claims', *Journal of Risk and Uncertainty,* 4, 4, 403–23.

Towse, A and Danzon, P (1999), 'Medical negligence and the NHS: an economic analysis', *Health Economics,* 8, 93–101.

Walshe, K and Dineen, M (1998), *Clinical Risk Management: Making a Difference?,* NHS Confederation.